The Anunnaki of Nibiru

Mankind's Forgotten Creators Enslavers, Saviors, and Hidden Architects of the New World Order

Gerald R. Clark

GERALD R. CLARK

DEDICATION

This book is dedicated to my wife and soul mate Christa. Her love and encouragement were necessary catalysts to delve deeply into the most fundamental truths facing mankind today.

Buy a copy of her book, *"The Artistic Vegan Meatless Mainstays for Modern Man"* available for sale on Amazon!

ACKNOWLEDGEMENTS

Inspiration to delve into the Sumerian history first arose while doing business in Turkey. Discovering cities that pre-dated the Egyptian pyramids, like Çatalhöyük, mentioned in Jared Diamond's Pulitzer Prize winning book "*Guns, Germs, and Steel*"[3], led my personal research to the earliest known writings of a civilized people, the Sumerians. Hebrew scholar and best-selling author Zecharia Sitchin, not only decoded the Sumerian cuneiform script, but did so with extensive references that satisfied even the most scrupulous Western modern academic and scientific mind. Great truths are being revealed to mankind thanks in great part to the research and published works of Zecharia Sitchin.

Table of Contents

List of Tables and Figures

1 PREFACE

Technical capabilities to include: building, transportation, and astronomy attributed to bygone civilizations are still a source of wonder for Westerners today. Innumerable television specials on the archeological findings relating to the Egyptian pyramids, the Mayan calendar, and discoveries of books and records from around the world uncovered in various forms, to include Sumerian Cuneiform tablets, provides modern man with a new understanding of ancient history. This lost knowledge has been slow to make its way into mainstream thought and is just now beginning to air on television on the History and Discovery Channels. It took time for archeologists to find the right artifacts to decode the past languages from the region.

Many historical and scriptural findings that were not included in or misrepresented by the Canonical Bible have now come to light. Access to scripts such as the Book of Enoch, the Nag Hamadi Gospels, the Book of Jubilees, among other historical texts, when synthesized and correlated with existing documents, is truly an eye opener relative to the common beliefs found in the modern Western culture.

Ancient Writings other than the books of the Canonical Bible broaden our knowledge base relative to history in the Middle East. Hidden scrolls tucked away in remote caves, cuneiform tablets covered by the sands of time, and equinox and solstice temples aligned perfectly to the sun lay forgotten in the deserted plains of Mesopotamia. Many of the documents predate the Canonical Bible by thousands of years, shedding light on the origins and influences of the familiar stories told therein having an immense influence on Western thought.

Would it surprise the reader to know that the flood hero Noah was actually a Sumerian King in the city of Shurrupak? He was quite well educated and wrote an account of his own regarding the times in which he lived. In the epic of Gilgamesh, one of the longest known stories involving the King of the Sumerian city of Uruk, the King visits Noah and has a long conversation with him about some issues common to both of them. Also from Sumeria, that is the Southern extreme of Mesopotamia—the land between the two rivers: the Tigris and Euphrates, hails the Biblical Patriarch Abraham. Abram became Abraham once the covenant is made between him and the Lord, prior to that he was called Abram. Recall in Genesis 12:1-4 where The Lord said to Abram,

Genesis 12:1-4 (NIV)

"Leave your country, your people and your father's household

and go to the land I will show you.

I will make you into a great nation and I will bless you.

I will make your name great, and you will be a blessing.

I will bless those that bless you and whoever curses you I will curse;

and all peoples on earth will be blessed through you."

Abram was in the Sumerian city of Haran when he received the call from the Lord to go to the land of Canaan. Note that Abram was born in the Sumerian city of Ur approximately 1433 BCE. His father, Terah, was an artisan and priest in the local temple, and his brothers Nahor and Haran resided in Ur as well [40]. We find Abraham in the city of Haran when he is preparing to leave for Canaan as stated in Genesis 15:7.

Genesis 15:7 (NIV)

"I am the Lord, who brought you out of Ur of the Chaldeans

to give you this land to take possession of it.

Wasn't the God of Abraham, Isaac, and Jacob the God of the Israelites, the God of the Old Testament? Thus, in addition to names like Jehovah, Yahweh, and El Sheddai, Abraham's God had another name in Sumer, one which he was called in one of his Temples in the city of Ur.

According to Cuneiform tablets found in Ur and many other pre and post-dilluvial cities along the Tigris and Euphrates to include Sippar and Nineveh, this Sumerian deity also had brothers and sisters who were also worshipped as gods in Mesopotamia and the surrounding regions. Abraham's deity's name is mentioned in other noteworthy documents from the region and era to include the Atrahasis, the Enuma Elish, and the Epic of Gilgamesh. Abraham and Noah also have close contact with these deities. Who were they and how do we know they existed? What are we to think about the fact that Abraham's God had a previous history as a Sumerian deity with a temple dedicated to him in Ur of the Chaldeans?

The funding for early archeological inquiries was closely controlled and channeled by early church authorities, in particular the Roman Catholic Church. A mandate was issued to only fund the archeological explorations that perpetuated the story told in the canonical Bible, established by the same institution at the Council of Nicea, 343 CE. Eventually, hidden books and suppressed artifacts, codices, cylinder seals, and Sumerian cuneiform inscribed monuments and tablets gave up their secrets to the inquisitive minds of disenfranchised seekers of truth.

A heroic gentleman comes to mind, discovered during the research into this book, a Major Henry Rawlings, responsible for recording and decoding three languages he discovered in 1835 located 1700 feet above the desert floor chiseled into the cliffs of Behistun, in modern day Iran. The historical marker was commissioned by Darius the 1st who lived and reigned from 522-486 BCE, recounting the Persian ruler's suppression of various rival uprisings. Major Rawling's copied the strange wedge-shaped writings etched into the sheer rock face and made them available to the British Museum after spending time decoding the tablets. His efforts lead to the ability to translate Old Persian, Elamite, and Akkadian scripts from one to the other leading to the re-discovery of the Mesopotamian sites in modern day Iraq, buried beneath the desert sands. A new investigation of the first-hand writings and evidence left by the Egyptians, Sumerians, and early church authors sheds new light on the historical truth, which at times seems stranger than the wildest contrived fictional tales. Discoveries at the ancient Mesopotamian cities of Nineveh all the way to the very Southern city of Eridu have many secrets to reveal, many of which are discussed in this book.

Various clues have surfaced and been laid bare for all to see, wrought forth by the dedication, sweat, and blood of the investigative pioneers from the past. It is now the responsibility for modern man to take a fresh look at the original evidence from which historians and scribes of the past aggregated the genesis accounts upon which our society's civilization foundations rest. Knowing that history's texts are inked by those in power at the time events are recorded, often relegates truth to the sidelines in favor of a story that perpetuates the controlling influences of the ruling party. Flagrant acts such as chipping away hieroglyphic evidence captured in stone to subsuming names and ranks of rival deities and creating also known as lists adds confusion to further cloud the truth.

Thus, given the unreliable nature of historical accuracy, people relegated the responsibility of knowing the truth to authorities appointed over them. This happened readily for those unfortunate enough to not be able to read-which throughout history included the majority. Scribes and priests were often those trained in the lingual arts and thus had their fingers on the pulse of truth throughout history. Books written by first-hand authors that told the truth, such as the Book of Enoch, were hidden from mankind for thousands of years and are now widely in circulation. Tens of thousands of Cuneiform inscribed tablets that lay forgotten; buried for thousands of years guarding recorded secrets hidden beneath the silt and sand of the Mesopotamian plains, recently unearthed all along the Tigris and Euphrates rivers, have been recovered and decoded by archeologists. So many tablets, tens of thousands, written in baked clay were recovered that the discovery spawned a cuneiform digitization project to expedite the process of garnering the tablet's secrets [63]. Many of the Sumerian artifacts and cuneiform tablets are on display in prominent museums in London, Paris, and Berlin to name just a few.

The oldest Sumerian records pre-date the books of the canonical Bible by thousands of years in some cases. The Sumerian records, discovered in cities like Uruk, the Biblical Erech, record mundane activities involving marriage and trade, and more important accounts of decrees and records of birth and death, etc. Referencing the first-hand historical accounts versus those composed by the societal victors, allows one to at least compare the current basis for cultural events and social mores with their antecedent counterparts from multiple recorded cultural perspectives toward a synthesized whole.

Stranger than fiction was the account of Noah's mystifying near-alien birth as described in vivid detail in the Book of Enoch [36]. According to some sources, Noah's father was definitely not Lamech as told in Genesis 5: 28, but rather one of the Mesopotamian deities that ends up saving him from the deluge [37]. The old Babylonian version of the flood account depicts the deity speaking to a reed hut where Ziusudra, *AKA* Noah, resides thereby divulging the urgent warning to get prepared for a flood that was to arrive on the Mesopotamian plains. This same story is told in the Bible sans illuminating Sumerian detail.

By analyzing the various birth accounts, genealogy tables, and deities venerated in the temples of Mesopotamia, an interesting realization, actually a profound epiphany is revealed! A cultural lie is uncovered that has such profound impact as to relegate all previous beliefs to obscurity, as if one had not come to that conclusion already given our present-day knowledge base. When asking a Westerner the simple question, *who was Yahweh?*, one gets the typical *AKA* list to include Jehovah and finally the *AKA* list ends with the answer of God, as taught intentionally with the help of the canonical Bible, in particular the Old Testament. When one realizes that one of the Gods of the Old Testament, Yahweh, was none other than the local deity of the Sumerian city of Ur, i.e. Enlil, the truth is revealed. For you see, Enlil was written about in a plethora of accounts in Sumeria and elsewhere in the region. Enlil and his relatives were venerated as gods in various temples from Nineveh to Assur to the Sumerian city of Ur to name just a few. Similarly his brother Enki and his children Nannar and Innana also had temples in prominent cultural and trade portals within the region. More importantly, Enlil was not acting alone, but rather in consort with others referred to as the Anunnaki in the Atrahasis or the Nephilim or Elohim in the Genesis 1:26 account wherein the confusing statement is made:

Genesis 1:26 (NIV)

Then God said, "Let us make man in our image, in our likeness..."

The confusion created by the plural statement "us, our" in the Biblical creation account is clarified when reading texts that predate the Genesis account by more than 1700 years such as the Atrahasis. Atrahasis, *AKA* the Biblical Noah, tells the story of the creation of man linking the same deities venerated in the temples of Mesopotamia with Enlil-Yahweh of the old testament and his brother Enki-Adonai: the hidden "us" in Genesis

1:26.   For Enki is mentioned along with his half-sister Ninmah, participating in genetic trials to produce a primitive worker, homo sapiens sapiens.

A very detailed account is provided of a clinical trial that results in the archetype for the human race Adam being birthed. The trial was conducted by Enlil's half-sister, Ninharsag or Ninmah, and his archrival and scientifically-inclined brother Enki, in an African laboratory. The historical records appeal to even the most scrutinizing scientist who recognizes readily the threshold of knowledge required to discuss a topic such as genetic engineering, in a document almost five thousand years old, which provides a more detailed account of the creation of man; one that makes sense technically and historically versus the précis version provided in the Bible, although in many cases complementary. Additionally, similar records illuminate the life of King Ut-napishtim of Shurrupak, the Biblical Noah, said to be 600 years old at the time of the great flood.

It seemed that various deities had *also known as* (AKA) names which seemed to span long periods of time. The great god Sin, as named by the Akkadians, after whom the Sinai peninsula was named, had an *AKA* name linking him to various Sumerian cities such as Ur and Harran: where he was known as Nannar the moon god, son of Enlil. His sister, Inanna also sported the symbol of the crescent moon and had temples throughout Mesopotamia. She was known as Ishtar to the Akkadians.

The Greek historian Herodotus lived in the 5th century BCE and hailed from Ionia. He delineated the Egyptian civilization into three dynasties and the model is still used by Egyptologists today. Manetho, the Egyptian priest-historian appears to have agreed with Herodotus partitioning the Egypt ruler ship, with the exception that instead of 3 dynasties, he included an additional era that was ruled by the gods alone. Manetho states that the first dynastic rulers of Egyptian gods ruled for 12,300 years [16] :

1st Egyptian Dynasty Ruler	Reign (years)
Ptah	9,000
Ra	1,000
Shu	700
Geb	500
Osiris	450
Seth	350
Horus	300

Table 1: First Dynasty of Egypt

Again, we find astonishingly long reigns listed in Table 1 above for the First Egyptian Dynasty rulers. It is interesting to note that in the Sumerian texts, Enki, a high-ranking deity from the city of Eridu, was assigned the regions of Egypt and Africa by his father Anu, on or before 3760 BCE. It just so happens that the Jewish calendar, whose origins are from the Sumerian city of Nippur, begins its count in 3760 BCE as well. Coincidence you might be thinking, but not according to the ancient cuneiform texts.

The second Egyptian dynastic period, according to Manetho, was composed of twelve divine rulers that reigned for 1,570 years. The first god that ruled the second dynasty of gods was Thoth, who, it turns out, is also a son of Enki.

Next, Egypt was ruled by thirty demigods whose reign lasted for 3,650 years in total. Later, the Pharaonic dynasty, which scholars believe began approximately 3100 BCE, lasted for 350 years and was headquartered at Men-Nefer, or Memphis in Greek.

Who were these deities? Clues to the mystery are further confounded when viewing the Sumerian King's List. Some of the reigns for the first kings in Sumer lasted up to 28,800 years according to the records. This is quite difficult to believe. The Sumerians claimed that all aspects of civilization were taught to them by the deities that were worshipped in the temples of Mesopotamia. Detailed knowledge about the orbital plane, tilt axis, spherical shape, and precessional behavior of the earth's equinox were known by the Sumerian deities, who were also credited for creation of the Zodiac. Contrast this detailed level of knowledge in Sumer with that possessed in Europe during the *Middle-Ages*. Scientists and church authorities in Europe were at odds whether the earth was round or flat while the peoples of Sumer and the surrounding region had advanced mathematics, metallurgy, law codes, and produced many of civilizations first inventions and advanced achievements [41].

A female Sumerian deity, Inanna, was also known as Hathor in Egypt and her name is well recognized and memorialized on the walls of temples to include the Temple of Hathor found on Mount Serabit El Khadim, the Biblical Mount Sinai; the mountain in the wilderness of the deity Nannar-Sin. The deity Sin is also described in various traditions to include Assyria, and those cultures that associate with the crescent moon symbol found on flags and mosques affiliated with the religion of Islam. The male deity recognized as the moon god to the peoples of Mesopotamia was Nannar-Sin who also had a sister, none other than the goddess Inanna *aka* Hathor to the Egyptians. From the genealogy accounts inscribed in baked clay on display in museums throughout the world the authors readily proclaimed in the Sumerian records, Nannar-Sin was the son of Enlil, and was also known as the moon god to peoples of the ancient Middle East. There are links in historical texts indicating that Nannar-Sin had a very large following in his cult centers that were prolific in the area from southern Iraq to Syria, Turkey and Iran. Interestingly enough, the Kaba stone in Mecca, Saudi Arabia, one of the sacred centers for the religion of Islam, was originally dedicated to the moon god, referred to there as Allah. Could Nannar-Sin be the deity that Mohammed had an encounter with in the wilderness? Is Nannar-Sin the fabled Allah?

At this historical juncture, the very instance one proper noun replaces another, especially as it relates to a deity's name; a new epithet begins as an old one is occluded or subsumed. Witnessing the Sumerian deity Enlil whose origins were mysterious but had been recorded and witnessed daily by the Biblical patriarch Abraham and peoples of the city of Ur, become the lofty one of the mountain, El Shaddai and eventually Jehovah to the people of the land of Israel, was an astounding discovery that linked the deities of Sumeria with at least one God of the old testament. This fact becomes apparent when comparing the Sumerian Storm God (Enlil) written about in the Lamentations of Ur with the God of wrath and vengeance of the Old Testament. More personable Gods were worshipped elsewhere in the region: like Enki, aka Ahura Mazda as he was known in ancient Persia, the "creator of all good things, god of light and wisdom" Ahura Mazda was replaced by Allah, aka Nannar-Sin when Arab conquerors overtook the Persians in 633 BCE, headquartered at their spectacular capital at Persepolis. The Arab incursion led to the decline of the Zoroastrian religion with the ending of the Sassanid Empire in 644 BCE.

Subsumption of names and epithets was a common practice performed by Egyptian and Sumerian cultures to solidify power and authority. This was a method used to coalesce multiple namesakes into a single name, one that was crafted to fit the culture and language used by the worshipping subjects, probably for ease of reference and aggregation of rivals when convenient.

When one realizes with full force that what one culture calls a deity is then termed by another name in a follow-on culture that the idea of a cultural myth takes on more significance, especially if the name is traceable cross-culturally. See God Table 9. For just as the purveyor of truth in history are hand-selected by the victors, the validity of a belief whether political or religious is perpetuated in a society by the same governing forces. Thus what the victor believes is **truth**; what others believe is politely termed *myth* instead of the politically incorrect label of lie. Similarly, when discussing religious truth, there is what the ruling party or superpower believes and what the subordinated cultures believe which is given a derogatory label as *pagan* or *occult*. A horribly relevant example of this is taking place and manifesting presently in the Middle East where the religious factions representing Christianity, Judaism, and Islam are waging war in the ancient land of Canaan, near Mount Megiddo located approximately 15 miles south of Haifa, Israel. Warring factions whose genealogy derives from rival deities originating in Sumeria are still in conflict today. The devotees of Enlil, *AKA* Yahweh the God of the Old

Testament, stand toe to toe with the followers of Enki-Poseidon, apparently still at odds with each other over dominion of the earth. Could the conflicts involving the countries of Iran, Iraq, Syria and Israel be a result of the past wars that took place between Enlil and Enki and their offspring as written about in the "Wars of Gods and Men" by Zecharia Sitchin? Whether truth or fiction, dogma or doctrine, the armies of the generals of the earth are gathered together once again in the Middle East where the nuclear countdown clock is just about out of time. Will the offspring of Enki interrupt the destructive plan his arch rival Enlil (Zeus to the Greeks) along with his warring son Ninurta (Apollo to the Greeks). *Is it possible that the reason the Jewish people reject Jesus as the Messiah is because he was the offspring of Enki, Jehovah's rival?* These and many more profoundly important topics are explored with the reader in this book.

2 SUMERIAN HISTORY

According to the interpretations of Sumerologists, the term AN.UNNA.KI literally is interpreted as those who from "heaven to earth came." The key point to note early on is the affiliation of the term "Heaven" with the claimed planet of Anunnaki origin, namely Nibiru as detailed in "The 12th Planet", written by Sitchin in 1976. Additionally, from the list of characters detailed as "deities" in Mesopotamian literature like the "Epic of Gilgamesh", we know that the head of the Anunnaki council of 12 was chaired by Anu, the father of the two key players and half brothers Enlil and Enki. Figure 1 below depicts the council composition as of 3760 BCE.

From the digitized cuneiform script, one can compose the word NI.BI.RU from three syllables which are listed in the Unicode as 1224C, 12249, and 12292.

1224C   12249   12292

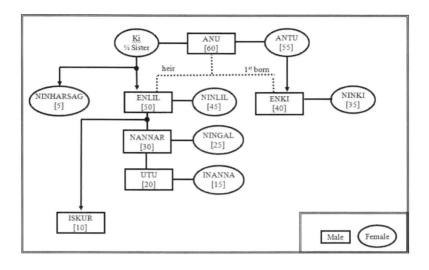

Figure 1: Anunnaki Council of Twelve on Earth 3760 BCE

Thus, a more accurate interpretation of the word Anunnaki is those who from Anu to the Earth came or was sent. *Annuna* is a self-referenced term Enlil uses for their race in the Atrahasis on the Mount Ararat encounter with Ziusudra. Thus, an alternative way of spelling it would be Annua.Ki, specifying a different set of Uniform Hexadecimal codes allocated to the Cuneiform Script as shown for the spelling of Nibiru previously. Equating the planet Nibiru with the word Heaven, as used in the Bible, is an important detail when re-examining prayers like "Our Father who art in Heaven…", shining a whole new light on who the Father in Heaven actually was, namely Anu. Thus the prayer must have originated among one of his kids on Earth, Enlil, Enki, or Ninmah or Ninharsag as depicted in Figure 1 above.

What was the reason that the Anunnaki left Nibiru to come to the Earth? Nibiru, located beyond Pluto in our Solar System, is trapped in a 3600-year retrograde elliptical orbit around our sun. According to maps found in Sumeria, and reports from the 1986 IRAS Naval Observatory discovery of a brown dwarf in the region Nibiru was reported to reside by the Sumerians, and the intense Catholic focus on Mount Graham using the *Lucifer* scope watching for Nibiru's arrival, the planet is real.

So, what prompted an advanced civilization on Nibiru to send a team of exploratory scientists to Earth? According to the genealogy table shown in Figure 2 below, various political struggles for power were ongoing with environmental pressures garnering the attention of the governing council on Nibiru. For those with diminishing eyesight, Figure 2 is reproduced as a full size drawing, for ease of reference in Appendix A.

The ANUNNAKI OF NIBIRU

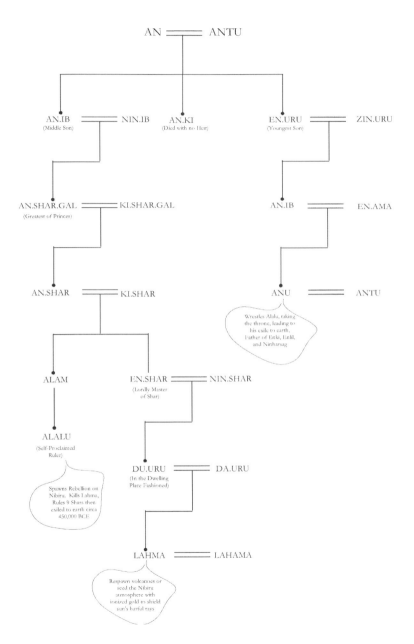

Figure 2: Anu Family History on Nibiru

Brown dwarf planets, as we know, do not receive significant solar radiation sufficient to keep the surface temperature habitable, as is the case for Earth given its optimal distance from the sun. The atmosphere on Nibiru was generated either artificially or from gasses and released steam from the geo-thermally heated planet. Consider the periodic exposure of an outer planet that normally receives very low levels of direct solar radiation in its outer orbit but intense exposure during the close perigee when the atmosphere would receive a larger radiation dose. According to Sitchin's published history timeline [88] approximately 450,000 years ago, life on Nibiru was facing extinction due to a deteriorating atmosphere and the subsequent exposure to radiation, especially at close perigee with the sun. This event is depicted in Figure 2 shown in the dialog box at the bottom left hand side.

A political struggle was also taking place on Nibiru, wherein Anu succeeds in wresting kingship from the unjust ruler Alalu, leading to his exile. Alalu escapes in a space craft in anticipation of his exile sentencing and subsequently discovers gold on Earth. Alalu's precious metal discovery is offered as an amend to save Nibiru's failing atmosphere by dispersing ionized gold particles into the home planet's degrading atmosphere.

Anu dispatches his premier scientifically-minded son Enki to assess the possibility of recovering Alalu's reported gold from Earth. Enki departs for Earth approximately 5,000 earth years later 445,000 ago, noting that a Niburian year is equal to 3,600 earth years. According to Sumerian records, to include the Sumerian King's list, the first city colonized by the Anunnaki was Eridu, located at the headwaters of the Persian Gulf [16]. Following their arrival on Earth, Enki, along with a small band of support staff, began prospecting for gold in the waters of the Gulf, with limited success. The lack of progress in producing a sufficient amounts of gold to repair the ailing atmosphere prompts Anu to send his younger son, Enlil, to help Enki speed up the gold recovery process. The mining operation was being transitioned from the waters of the Persian Gulf to mining the ore located by Enki in South Africa, in the vicinity of the Zambezi River. Given the support infrastructure that would be needed to crush rock and process gold-laden ore, Enki and Enlil invited Anu to come to Earth and provide council on the arduous mining task.

Between approximately 445,000 to 360,000 years ago, Anu arrived on Earth and was briefed on the current gold mining operational status that his son Enki was spearheading. A question of which brother should handle the mining operation in Africa and which would head up the command headquarters in Mesopotamia, specifically in Nippur, was at issue. According to the Atrahasis account, Anu, Enlil, and Enki drew lots to determine which mission each would pursue separately, creating space between the two half brothers that were often at odds. Enki was the first born son to Anu and Antu. Enlil was, according to the Sumerian accounts, the rightful heir. Based on Niburian inheritance rules, the rightful heir is designated as the offspring of the male and his half-sister. The reason this was done by the Anunnaki was rooted in science. The female contribution to the genetic material includes mitochondrial DNA which the male does not. This predisposes the genetic blood line toward the maternal source.

Following the drawing of lots, Enlil was assigned to the Mesopotamian region where he would eventually be served by Terah and his son Abram in the temple at Ur. Enki was assigned to the Abzu (Africa) to speed up the gold mining operation badly needed to repair the Niburian degenerating atmosphere. Anu returned to Nibiru to run the kingship back on the home planet. Innana, Anu's favorite granddaughter, was given the Indus Valley region, and the Sinai Peninsula was retained for use by the Anunnaki. The division took place and was finalized in the calendar year 3760 BCE.

Approximately 415,000 years ago, Enki's half sister Ninharsag, a medical officer, traveled to Earth and established her medical center at Shurrupak. Her mission was to provide health care support for the space traveling Niburian astronauts. There were complaints from the Anunnaki about noticeable aging effects that were not seen on Nibiru. It was postulated that the more rapid circuits they were experiencing on Earth versus Nibiru with a much slower circuit, namely a 3,600 year "shar".

City	Function
Nippur	Mission Control Center
Sippar	Space Port
Shurrupak	Medical Center
Bad Tibira	Gold Ore Processing
Larsa and Lagash	Navigational Aids
Ur	Command Headquarters, Enlil
Eridu	Earth Station One, Enki HQ

Table 2: Pre-Dilluvial Anunnaki Outposts

Several cities were established in Sumeria, augmenting the existing Eridu built by Enki upon his prior arrival. These cities were designed to provide specific functions related to the mining operation and subsequent ore processing as well as the infrastructure needed to remain in communications with Nibiru [13]. Table 2 depicts the cities and their respective functions. Figure 3 shows a relational city map.

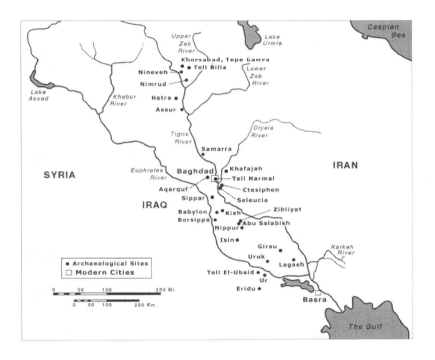

Figure 3: Pre-Dilluvial Anunnaki Cities in Mesopotamia

As told in the Atrahasis, approximately 300,000 years ago in Enki's domain in Southern Africa, the Anunnaki Council of 12 met to discuss how to increase gold production rates. Background information from the account sets the scene for the ancient astronaut's noteworthy recorded historical event. The higher ranking members of the Anunnaki Council, purportedly Enki himself, brought several subservient workers to help with establishing the gold mining outpost on Earth. The Lost Book of Enoch refers to them as Watchers [36], but the Atrahasis calls the miners Igigi. They were apparently very advanced relative to humans, although designated the working class agent. Fig 3 depicts archeological sties in Mesopotamia.

Difficult labor-intensive tasks were assigned to the Igigi, to include dredging rivers, digging and constructing aqua ducts, building cities and last, but not least, mining gold-bearing ore in Southern Africa. Apparently, they were not supplied with female companions during their alien deployment to Earth mining over a long period of time, measured in Niburian orbit lengths as a "shar" equaling 3,600 Earth years. What follows is an excerpt from the first tablet from the Atrahasis, the Old Babylonian Version (OBV) as translated by Stephanie Dalley in her Oxford World's Classics book entitled *"Myths From Mesopotamia: Creation, the Flood, Gilgamesh, and Others",[37] pages 9-10.*

Atrahasis Tablet 1 [37, pg 9]

When the gods instead of man

Did the work, bore the loads,

The gods' load was too great,

The work too hard, the trouble too much,

The great Anunnaki made the Igigi

Carry the workload sevenfold.

Anu their father was king,

Their counselor warrior Ellil,

Their chamberlain was Ninurta,

Their canal-controller Ennugi.

They took the box of lots...,

Cast the lots; the gods made the division.

Anu went up to the sky,

And Ellil took the earth for his people.

The bolt which bars the sea

Was assigned to far-sighted Enki.

When Anu had gone up the sky,

And the gods of the Apsu had gone below,

The Anunnaki of the sky

Made the Igigi bear the workload.

The gods had to dig out canals,

Had to clear channels, the lifelines of the land,

The Igigi had to dig out canals,

Had to clear channels, the lifelines of the land.

The gods dug out the Tigris river bed

And then dug out the Euphrates....

In the deep they set up

The Apsu of the land

Inside it raised its top

Of all the mountains

They were counting the years of loads;

For 3,600 years they bore the excess,

Hard work, night and day.

They groaned and blamed each other.
Grumbled over the masses of excavated soil.
"Let us confront the chamberlains,
And get him to relieve us of our hard work!"

With mutiny in the air, summarizing the key points of the first tablet, the Igigi surround Enlil's encampment (Ellil in the OBV translation) and demand to be relieved of their excessive work load. Anu, Enlil and Enki's father on Nibiru is summoned for his advice and counsel. Enki is also invited to help to come up with a resolution to the unrest in the mines. The Igigi are temporarily appeased with promises of work relief while the Anunnaki Council meets to discuss the rioting Igigi gold miners. Enki and Ninharsag, his half-sister and Chief Medical Officer, team up to develop a genetic hybrid being, a primitive worker, to replace the Igigi gold diggers. Next chapter the evidence supporting the Anunnaki on earth is explored with the reader.

3 EVIDENCE OF ANUNNAKI ON EARTH

What evidence is there that the Anunnaki were physically here on Earth? Evidence categories examined include Astrological, technical, documentary, and biological evidence.

Astrological Evidence

The Sumerian creation tale, as recorded on the Enuma Elish [89] clay tablets on display at the University of Pennsylvania Museum, is told as an allegory of celestial warriors whose skirmishes and exploits lead to the planets and their hosts established circuits around the sun. The Old Babylonian Version (OBV) of the clay tablets that record the Cuneiform inscribed tale, were dated to approximately 1936-1901 BCE. According to the Sumerian records, Marduk, first born son of Enki, was the national deity of Babylon, and was at the height of his reign at approximately 2000 BCE.

It is proffered that a much older version of the creation tale is in existence, which had Nibiru named as the home planet, Nibiru, which was replaced by the name Marduk in the OBV. The names of the planets and their orbital distance from the sun are accurately depicted, with exceptions. What is amazing about the Babylonian creation account is the advanced knowledge of our solar system that has only recently been verified by modern science. Is it possible that current scientific knowledge is only now maturing to the point that we can validate the Babylonian Epic of Creation?

The account specifies ten versus nine planets and includes the sun and moon among the hosts. Table 3 below depicts the our solar system planets and the Niburian names assigned to them. Note also that the Anunnaki elite have planets associated with their namesake and there were a total of 10 planets, versus our current understanding and acceptance of only 9, according to the Sumerian records.

Rank	Celestial Body	Epic of Creation Name
11	Sun	Apsu
10	Moon	Qingu
9	Mercury	Mummu
8	Venus	Lahamu
7	Earth	Ki
6	Mars	Lahmu
5	Jupiter	Kishar
4	Saturn	Anshar
3	Neptune	Nudimud
2	Uranus	Anu
1	Pluto	Gaga
12	Nibiru	Marduk

Table 3: Babylonian Epic of Creation Planets

Below is a summarized accounting of the Epic of Creation. The story begins with the Sun and Mercury conspiring to destroy Tiamut. Enki learns of the plot and shields Mercury by quelling the Sun's radiation. Enki then puts Mercury to "sleep" [37, p235] Enki puts the sun to sleep as well. Mercury, the counselor was in a sleepless daze. Ea (another name for Enki) unfastened his belt, took off his crown, then took away his mantel of radiance and put it on himself. Note that Enki's planet is Neptune and could be inferring that Mercury's orbit was temporarily changed while dealing with the solar radiation issue from the Sun. Nibiru rested on top of the sun for 900 years (captured in the sun's orbit?) [33]. the sun's solar radiation disturbs Tiamut, Ea and his wife Damkina have offspring, namely their firstborn son Marduk. Herein, Marduk takes liberty with the account as the progeny of the high ranking members of the Anunnaki Council, establishing his birthright spawned in the heavens. Marduk took over the council rank of 50 from Enlil at the height of his rule in Babylon.

The signs of the Zodiac in the Heavens are described to include Taurus, Pices, and Capricorn. Qingu (currently the Earth's moon) was aligned with Tiamut, which held the tablet of destinies. Neptune attempts to quell Tiamut's fury, stirred by the Sun, turning back and reporting to Anshar (Saturn). This forces Tiamut to stray from its orbital path. Ea recommends disbanding Tiamut's forces and volunteers Marduk (Nibiru) to help. Nibiru is drawn into Saturn's orbit, providing a calming effect. A satellite or moon of Saturn is sent to Mercury and Venus as a probe, whereby Mercury and Venus are alluded to as ancestors of Saturn. A Radiation weapon termed inhullu-wind is alluded to as an evil wind, the tempest, the whirlwind that releases 7 winds against Tiamut, advancing behind in Tiamut's path. A flood weapon is used against Tiamut, as an asteroid (arrow) hits Tiamut splitting it open. Subsequently, Qingu is destroyed. A constellation of planets, stars, and remnants of Tiamut are captured in Nibiru's orbit. The lower part of Tiamut is trampled, sending one half of its mass to the roof of the sky, drawing a bolt across it and a guard to hold it. Then the waters were arranged so they coagulated to an ocean. Nibiru's course was then corrected, and the location affixed to the stand of Enlil (planetary affiliation is Jupiter, Zodiac symbol of Taurus) and the stand of Enki (Zodiac affiliation Pices, Planetary Affiliation is Neptune). The Earth's moon was previously a moon of Tiamut.

The reader would be well served to read the Enuma Elish in its original form to get a sense of the detailed creation epic. From this allegorical account at the point of creation in our solar system, Tiamut, a planet the size of Uranus, had an established orbit between Mars and Jupiter. Earth had not come into existence at that time. Nibiru was somehow captured into our solar system's orbit, with various hypothesis about whence it came. This capturing started the celestial battle for orbital position if you will. When Nibiru entered its orbital path around the sun, passing the outer planets introduced gravitational forces that tilted Uranus on its side and dislodged Pluto from its orbit around Saturn, promoting it to *planethood* only to be demoted recently by the scientific community.

Then, one of Nibiru's satellites strikes Tiamut enroute to solar perigee and on its next orbital path Nibiru hit Tiamut directly. A large part of Tiamut broke off and became the Earth, with the left over debris becoming the asteroid belt, currently located between Mars and Jupiter. The Earth congealed into a solid planet in its current orbit capturing a moon of Nibiru as its own. Some modern scientific analysis of the earth's deep rifts in the Pacific as well as its unusually large size moon have been corroborated with the Sumerian creation account read every spring in Babylon. An impact from Nibiru could also have transferred the seeds of life to Earth, a form of accidental Panspermia versus the intentional one proposed by Dr. Jonas Salk of San Diego, suggesting that intelligent beings intentionally seeded planet Earth with alien life forms.

The most important part of the Epic of Creation specifies one additional planet in our solar system, the Anunnaki's home planet of Nibiru, whose apogee is positioned beyond Pluto in a 3,600 year retrograde orbit around the sun. Corroborating evidence was provided by the former chief of the U.S. Naval Observatory, Dr. Robert S. Harrington. A gent named Tombaugh discovered Pluto in 1930 and its moon Charon was found in 1978. Planetary wobbles in the orbital paths of Uranus and Neptune spawned the use of an infra-red astronomical satellite, IRAS in 1983 to locate the suspected planet that induced the wobbles. *The IRAS produced results indicating a large brown dwarf, four times the size of the Earth, had been located, without question.*

A newspaper article was published in 1992 by Harrington and Van Flandern of the Naval Observatory, working with all the information they had at hand, publishing their findings and opinion that a tenth planet had been located in our solar system, even calling it an intruder planet. [82] Zecharia Sitchin and Dr. Harrington, being familiar with all Sitchin's writings about a tenth planet, met to correlate the IRAS findings with the account he had interpreted from the Babylonian Epic of Creation, the Enuma Elish. Given the evidence reported by the IRAS, other space probes like Pioneer 10 and 11, Voyager, and the corroborating orbital path, planet size, and retrograde characteristics of the tenth planet, Harrington agreed with Sitchin that it was Nibiru[82]

The passage of a planet as large as Nibiru between Mars and Jupiter would certainly have a noticeable impact every 3,600 years. *It is highly probably that Nibiru's passage may be responsible for pole shifts and reversals, changes in the Earth's precession about its axis, and potentially dangerous meteors and space debris drug along from the asteroid belt inbound to perigee.*

Technological and Building Evidence

Unusual artifacts found around the world, those that seem to contradict the known abilities of the civilization under analysis, are not hard to find. Examples include hieroglyphs from the Egyptian temple of Abydos depicting rockets, airplanes, submarines, and even an advanced helicopter that looks similar to the United States AH-64 Apache Helicopter. There is also the Iraqi battery find, precision stone masonry and architecture using megalithic stones. Of all the building materials accessible to a culture, why choose the most difficult material possible? Massive 1000 ton plus stone blocks? The trilithon stones of Baalbek, Lebanon come to mind. The answer is more than likely because they could and it was easy for them.

One of the most intriguing finds was the temple of Hathor atop the Biblical Mount Sinai. Within the temple was found a strange white talcum powder that was apparently the result of smelting gold as it turned out [48]. This find led to the re-discovery of mono-atomic gold by David Hudson. These room temperature superconductors have anti-gravity properties and have been postulated to have been leveraged to move the large stone blocks used in temple construction. Additionally, there is clear evidence that the Anunnaki of a chosen blood line, were ingesting the mono-atomic gold in the form of conical bread cakes as depicted on Hathor's temple walls[48]. The shorter orbital cycles on Earth were having a negative effect on the Anunnaki DNA; specifically the telomeres were being damaged by close proximal radiation from the sun [14,16] The ingestion of mono-atomic gold has the effect of "lighting up" the human energy body as well as provisioning a bridge to other dimensions due to the missing atomic mass of the multi-pass annealing process applied to the smelting gold. Other ingredients were added to the gold to cause it to turn into a white powder and lose its mass, mainly Antimony.

Findings from around the world to include model airplanes, incredibly sophisticated solar and lunar temples aligned to solstice and equinox alike, along with tens of thousands of clay tablets and written accounts of advanced beings teaching civilizing technologies to indigenous peoples points overwhelmingly to the fact that the Anunnaki were here on Earth.

Impressive remnants left behind by the ancient Anunnaki astronauts are the structures in the pre-dilluvial cities in Mesopotamia such as Eridu, Babylon, and Uruk where the famed Gilgamesh was King.

Evidence List:
1. Building structures like Baalbek defy current engineering abilities [70].
2. Gold mines carbon dated to the period that Enki was said to be in Africa approximately 200,000 years ago[13,14].

3. Stone dwellings occupied by Mankind's true ancestors, Anunnaki genetic slaves, found by Michael Tellinger near the gold mining operation. Awaiting verifiable bodies found with DNA testing [111], queued up yet Michael?

4. Cuneiform baked clay tablets documenting who the Anunnaki were, their mission, and their personalities are in the Sumerian record [41, 43].

5. Enuma Elish, on display in the University of Pennsylvania museum, has very sophisticated and technically accurate description of celestial collisions that led to the composition of our current solar system. In this depiction, Sumerians knew about Pluto that took NASA until 1980s to positively identify the planet. How did they know this [37, 89]?

6. City of Eridu photographed by University of Chicago in 1973 with its baked bricks protruding out of the Iraqi desert sands. Earth Station One located. City and King corroborated by the Sumerian King's List.

Documentary Evidence

Our understanding of the reality of those dwelling in the ancient Middle East did not come to light until the early 1800's. Archeological digs in Mesopotamia brought to the world's attention the sophistication of the Sumerians. Mixed in with ordinary civil records of marriage, birth, and legal contracts was evidence of the history of the Anunnaki themselves [116] !!! The Sumerians did not invent the concept of a mythological entity, but rather found in those records that the Sumerians knew the astronauts were not from Earth and were elevated as gods in the various cities where they took up residence in Ziggurat Temples. The aliens that setup the Sumer civilization were real flesh and blood who routinely interacted with the people, their genetic underling creation. Ashurbanipal's library at Nineveh was torched, firing many of the clay tablets therein, preserving them for antiquity. Recently a sealed nine by six foot room in the Anunnaki space port of Sippar was found. Within the sealed chamber were nearly 400 chronologically ordered clay tablets which detailed the unbroken record of the Anunnaki's travails during mission Earth [82]. Sitchin was instrumental in getting the Sumerian details about the Anunnaki records for the world to see. It has taken over 100 years for the information to be accepted thus far. Tablets are now digitized for translation speed and accuracy [63].

Physical evidence that correlates to the documentary evidence is not hard to find either. The Sumerian Atrahasis document indicates that the Anunnaki were mining gold in Africa. Those ancient mines have been found and carbon dated, indicating they could have been in used by 200,000 year old miners with links to our true biological ancestors according to Michael Tellinger, author of "Adam's Calendar" [111] and the "Slave Species of God" [119]. The catalyst for Michael's search in South Africa for the Anunnaki gold mines came from texts like the Atrahasis and the Sumerian record pointing to Africa, Enki's domain.

Biological-Genetic Evidence

It should not surprise the reader that the genetic evidence indicating that the first primitive workers that the Anunnaki developed took place in South Africa in close proximity to the gold mines that were purchased by the Anglo American plc, a mining corporation [112]. Enki's house of Shimti, his genetics lab, is in exactly the same location where the Genetic Eve study tracking mitochondrial DNA specified it would be [86,88]. This was also corroborated by the Genetic Adam study tracking the mutation of the Ychromosome, leading to the same area and time frame as the Genetic Eve study. The Atrahasis provides several details about mixing animal, and Anunnaki DNA until the final solution was found, homo sapiens sapiens [37].

The intelligence that the Anunnaki stated that mankind received accounts for our out of place and time rapid technological developments that have seen advanced space travel after only 200,000 or so years of evolution. This does not jive well with the record on how tool progress iteratively occurred over millions of years, versus rapid paradigm shifts like that of the Sumerians forward [43]. In the next chapter, we will take a closer look at mankind's genetic creator.

4 ENKI THE SCIENTIST: MAN'S CREATOR

The Anunnaki found themselves in a considerable bind conducting the mining operations in South Africa. After arriving with Enki almost 432,000 years ago, the Igigi helped colonize the Earth. After splashing down in the Persian Gulf, building Eridu (Earth Station One) and attempting to unsuccessfully glean sufficient quantities of gold from the ocean, the mining operation was moved the Abzu (Africa) along the Zambezi River. The Igigi were later accompanied by lower echelon workers that were dedicated to the gold ore mining task. After long periods working in the mines, under what appears to be harsh conditions, the miners rebelled surrounding Enlil's fortress, and demanded relief.

The following passage from the Atrahasis captures the emotional mood the miners were in after, according to the account, working for 3,600 years (1 shar coincidentally = 1 Niburian Solar Year).

Atrahasis Tablet 1 [37, pg 10]

Come, let us carry Ellil,

The counselor of gods, the warrior, from his dwelling

Then Alla made his voice heard,

And spoke to the gods his brothers

Come! Let us carry Ellil,

The counselor of gods, the warrior, from his dwelling.

Now, cry battle!

The gods listened to his speech,

Set fire to their tools,

Put aside their spade for fire,

Their loads for the fire-god,

They flared up. When they reached

The gate of warrior Ellis's dwelling,

It was night, the middle watch,

The house was surrounded...

Enlil's guards, Nuksu and Kalkal, roused their master to the rabble that was surrounding his house. When Enlil was told he was surrounded by the Igigi miners, he had weapons brought to his dwelling. Nusku, Enlil's vizier, cautioned him to seek counsel from his father Anu and to also fetch Enki. Anu and Enki were summoned to an impromptu Council meeting to discuss what to do about the revolting lower echelon Anunnaki.

Atrahasis Tablet 1 [37, pg 10]

Anu king of the sky was present,

Enki king of the Apsu attended.

The great Anunnaki were present.

Ellil got up and the case was put.

Ellil made his voice heard

And spoke to the great gods,

"Is it against me that they have risen?

Shall I do battle...?

Anu made his voice heard

And spoke to the warrior Ellil,

"Let Nuksu go out

And find out word of the Igigi

Who have surrounded your door.

Nusku, fully armed, approached the rabble mob and queried on behalf of Anu, Enki, Enlil, and the canal-controller Ennugi who was in charge and what the problem was?

The revolting miners told Nusku to give Enlil the message:

Atrahasis Tablet 1 [37, pg 12]

"Every single one of us gods declared war!

We have put a stop to the digging.

The load is excessive, it is killing us!"

Upon hearing the issue presented by Nuksu on behalf of the fed up miners, Enlil wept upon hearing the news then turned to his father Anu and asked that one of the miners be made an example of by terminating him publicly.

Atrahasis Tablet 1 [37, pg 13-15]

Anu made his voice heard

And spoke to the gods his brothers,

"What are we complaining of?

Their work was indeed too hard, their trouble was too much.

Every day the earth resounded,

The warning signal was loud enough, we kept hearing the noise.

(gap)

Enki (Ea) made his voice heard

And spoke to the gods his brothers,

"Why are we blaming them?"

Their work was too hard, their trouble was too much.

(gap)

Belet-ili the womb-goddess is present—

Let her create primeval man

So that he may bear the yoke,

So that he may bear the work of Ellil,

Belet-ili the womb-goddess is present,

Let the womb-goddess create offspring,

And let man bear the load the gods!"

(gap)

Nintu (AKA: Belet-ili) made her voice heard,

And spoke to the great gods,

"It is not proper for me to make him.

The work is Enki's; He makes everything pure!

If he gives me clay, then I will do it"

Enki made his voice heard

And spoke to the great gods,

"On the first, seventh, and fifteenth of the month

I shall make a purification by washing.

Then one god should be slaughtered.

And the gods can be purified by immersion.

Nintu shall mix clay

With his flesh and blood.

Then a god and a man

Will be mixed together in clay.

Let us hear the drumbeat forever after,

Let a ghost come into existence form the god's flesh,

Let her proclaim it as his living sign,

And let the ghost exist so as not to forget the slain god.

They answered "Yes"!" in the assembly,

The great Anunnaki who assign the fates.

So, the Anunnaki council, with Anu as the head of the assembly, makes the decision to allocate Enki and Nintu (the medical officer also known as Ninharsag) to the task of creating a primitive worker to replace the rebellious Igigi miners. The Atrahasis continues in great detail describing the multiple genetic attempts, failures, and abominable mishaps. When success was finally at hand, Nintu, who was then promoted to Mistress of All Gods, spoke to the Anunnaki council.

Even the mother of mankind has to submit a "TPS" report to justify her accomplishment to her boss!

Atrahasis Tablet 1 [37, pg 16]

"I have carried out perfectly

The work that you ordered of me.

You have slaughtered a god together with his intelligence.

I have relieved you of your hard work.

I have imposed your load on man."

The concept of genetic manipulation is not only understood among modern civilized peoples today, but is so common that it is no big deal. Could it be true that the Anunnaki, at least 450,000 years ahead of our civilization and having conquered space travel, had the ability to do in-vitro fertilization? According to the Atrahasis account, they certainly did. This brings into serious question the idea of man's concept of a "creator". The question that comes to mind is whether the genetic scientist of our modern era is really any different functionally than that performed by Enki in his African lab? Note the Anunnaki concept of a spirit transferred from a sacrificed being to another. This coincides with stories of underworld energy/soul maintenance.

A point to consider from the Enuma Elish creation account is that the collision between Nibiru and Tiamut, a portion of which became the Earth, could have been contaminated with the seeds of life from Nibiru. These seeds of life, according to Enki's writings, were from the Creator of All. Thus, the Anunnaki had a meta-concept beyond that of a god, which even the Igigi were sometimes called. Enki stated that the bipedal hominids he found on the African plains were recognizable as a species based on the evolutionary process seen on Nibiru. Thus, the genetic upgrade given to early pre-human hominids was seen as a temporal head start program, not necessarily creating a new species all together.

Mankind had an original Creator of All to thank for the seeds of life, along with the ancient astronaut Enki whose genetic seed was used as the archetypal Adapa, the first human, bearing the mark of the Anunnaki. Our ancient astronaut identity and intelligence is resident in our hybrid Anunnaki genes.

A very important point is brought to the attention to the reader, given the known age of the Atrahasis tablets written during the Old Babylonian Period dated to 1700 BCE. The Sumerian flood account was clearly copied and modified to create the Genesis account, written by Hebrew priests being held captive in Babylon, where they had access to the true story of the great flood but chose to placate Enlil as their chosen monotheistic ancient astronaut god. After all, they were scared to death of Enlil's wrath. Genesis 6 describes the background scene of the great flood from the Enlilite perspective, having tried to eliminate all references to the other members of the Anunnaki council in the Torah narrative, especially any reference to his arch rival and half brother Enki.

Genesis 6:1-8 (NIV)

When men began to increase in number on the earth and daughters were born to them, the sons of God saw that the daughters of men were beautiful, and they married any of them they chose.

Then the Lord said, "My Spirit will not contend with man forever, for he is mortal; his days will **be a hundred and twenty years."**

The Nephilim were on the earth in those days—and also afterward—**when the sons of God went to the daughters of men and had children by them.** They were the heroes of old, men of renown.

The Atrahasis OBV account uses a very different catalyst that leads to the destructive flood than the Genesis reference. In the Sumerian account, Enlil is furious at mankind's noise and wants them silenced. In the Genesis 6:1-8 account, the fact that the Nephilim take human wives, potentially breaking galactic law by shacking up with a genetic slave, is ignored by Enlil choosing to base mankind's extinction tale on how evil men were as noted in the following Biblical account.

Genesis 6: 5 (NIV)

The Lord saw how great man's wickedness on the earth had become, and that **every** inclination of the thoughts of his heart was only evil **all** the time.

The Lord was grieved that **he had made man** on the earth, and his heart was filled with pain. So the Lord said, "I will wipe mankind, **whom I have created,** from the face of the earth...

It is interesting to compare the Genesis account with the Atrahasis account. Here are just a couple of the bald faced lies which should be clear to the most casual observer. First, Enlil was not involved in the creation of mankind, as he claims in Genesis 6:5. But rather Enki and Ninmah were solely responsible as evidenced in the Atrahasis, predating the Genesis account by at least 1,700 years. If mankind's thoughts were evil all the time, did that include the time they were toiling in the mines to get gold ore for Enlil? His true complaint in the Atrahasis account was repeatedly that mankind was noisy and he could not sleep. How about some earplugs? Hmm, too much trouble or was the idea of prolific offspring of his arch rival brother that had the potential to rise up against his authority was more likely the case. Using terms like *all* and *every* in Genesis 6:5 is a Boolean Logic no-no. Clearly the Biblical ghost writer (Enlil) was not trained in the scientific Boolean Logical rule set rules, or often communicated in absolutes as evidenced herein.

It's interesting to consider that the "plant of knowledge of good and evil" was present in Sumeria, the Eden, and utilized by the Anunnaki. Enlil-Jehovah tells Adapa in the garden of Eden that if he eats it he will die. Enki counteracts this lie and tells Adapa he will surely not die but instead become like one of us, the gods. Thus, there seems to be a transformational effect, at the DNA level produced by this plant that changes human consciousness. In any event, Enki tells the truth and is Demonized and symbolized as a snake, while Enlil lies, and promotes himself as God. This lie, the fact that Adam did not die but rather became aware of his nakedness, attests to the stated outcome that Enki provided as the real reason Enlil did not want the plant of the knowledge of good and evil consumed. It was about controlling the access to higher consciousness, frowned upon by Enlil.

What happened next were unforeseen genocidal actions initiated by Enlil. Apparently after 600 years of the primal man breeding program humans were prolific and noisy.

Atrahasis Tablet 1 [37, pg 18]

600 years, less than 600 passed,

And the country became too wide, the people too numerous.

The country was as noisy as a bellowing bull.

The God grew restless at their racket,

Ellil had to listen to their noise.

He addressed the great gods,

"The noise of mankind has become too much,

I am losing sleep over their racket.

Give the order that šuruppu-disease shall break out.

This appears to be the genesis of all out conflict between Enki and Enlil. Mankind was Enki's proud creation with the help of Ninharsag, successfully alleviating the gods from the toils of the African gold mines just as he promised. Of course Enki would take issue with an order to release some form of disease on the populace by his half-brother Enlil, whose obvious intent was to wipe out the source of the noise, namely mankind. There were other deep-seated sources of conflict between the two which will be addressed later in the book. These issues involved birthright, inheritance and official rank and titles.

The NIV Bible corroborates the timeline from the creation of the Adapa to the time that they were so numerous that Enlil wanted them terminated, namely 600 years, Noah's age at the time of the flood.

Genesis 7:11 (NIV)

In the six hundredth year of Noah's life, on the seventeenth day of the second month—on that day all the springs of the great deep burst forth, and the floodgates of the heavens were opened. And rain fell on the earth forty days and forty nights.

Atrahasis later contradicts the 40 day continuous rain, specifying only 7 days of rain in the Sumerian account. It is also interesting to question the ages shown in the Bible from Adam to Noah in Genesis 5. The phenomenal ages listed range up to 895 years for Mahalalel and 962 years for Jared. Could it be that the ages were simply exaggerated or could the Anunnaki blood line, at its more pure state before dilution after generational mixing with mankind, accounted for the exceptional ages mentioned therein? Another point worth noting is the genetic age constraint the Anunnaki placed on their primitive workers, providing them with the intelligence to follow instructions in the mines, but a short life to prevent overpopulation. As pointed out in Genesis 6:3, mankind was allotted a maximum of a 120 year lifespan. This coincides with the Atrahasis account. Checking online, the oldest person in recorded history was Ms. Jeanne Calment, a French woman who lived from 21 February, 1875 to 4 August, 1997. She was officially recorded to be 122 years, 164 days old. Looks like she broke the Anunnaki genetic mold by a small amount, namely 2 years and 164 days. Although, given the multitudes that have stepped foot on Earth, the 120 year genetic design target seems to have worked quite well.

The text towards the end of Atrahasis Tablet 1 establishes that a close relationship exists between Atrahasis and the great god Enki. From the genealogy table shown in [48, pg 316] and the Lost Book of Enoch [36], it is asserted that Atrahasis was none other than the offspring of Enki and Batanash, the wife of the Biblical Lamech [14]. That being said, Enki coordinates a rebellion among mankind with Atrahasis his son, providing instructions as to how to perform a peaceful protest and shame the powers that be (Enlil) into ceasing the punishment by süruppu-disease, whatever that ailment was. Enki's intercession appears to have worked, much to Enlil's chagrin, clenching his jaw in preparation for the next onslaught against human fodder. Enlil orders a new genocidal tactic:

Atrahasis Tablet 1 [37, pg 20]

He addressed the great gods. (Elil= Enlil)

"The noise of mankind has become too much, I am losing sleep over their racket.

Cut off food supplies to the people!

Let the vegetation be too scant for their hunger!

Let Adad wipe away his rain. (Iskur Adad is one of Enlil's sons)

Below, let no flood-water flow from the springs.

Let wind go, let it strip the ground bare,

Let clouds gather but not drop rain,

Let the field yield a diminished harvest,

Let Nissaba stop up her bosom.

No happiness shall come to them."

Again, Enki runs intercession on behalf of the people, coaching them how to deal with the ill will of his half brother, Enlil. Enki instructs the people to resist by not praying to their goddess and shaming Iskur Adad for averting rain for the crops. Enki's intercession works again, but not for long. Enlil persists in his multi-pronged approach to wipe out mankind. He sends additional diseases to put an end to their noise. Mankind was summarily afflicted with sickness, headaches, and süruppu and asakku disease.

Atrahasis Tablet 1 [37, pg 26)

The field decreased its yield, Nissaba turned away her breast,

The dark fields became white,

The broad countryside bred alkali,

Earth clamped down her teats:

No vegetation sprouted, no grain grew.

Asakku was inflicted on the people,

The womb was too tight to let a baby out.

(gap)

When the second year arrived

They had depleted the storehouse.

When the third year arrived,

The people's looks were changed by starvation.

When the fourth year arrived

Their upstanding bearing bowed,

Their well-set shoulders slouched,

People went out in public hunched over.

When the fifth year arrived,

A daughter would eye her mother coming in;

A mother would not even open her door to her daughter.

A daughter would watch the scales at the sale of her mother,

A mother would watch the scales at the sale of her daughter,

When the sixth year arrived

They served up a daughter for a meal,

Served up a son for food.

Atrahasis seeks out his lord Enki yet again to protect himself and what is left of mankind against the genocidal onslaught that Enlil has brought to bear. This request for intercession once again leads to conflict between the two brothers. Enlil, still not satisfied with the destruction and disease he has brought to fruition against mankind, orders Enki to cause a flood to wipe out the remaining humans. Enki refuses angrily. Although the Anunnaki had the ability to manipulate the weather with a system like HAARP, it is not clear in these circumstances that the great flood to come was caused by the Anunnaki, but rather by gravitational forces wrought by Nibiru's passing Earth, enroute to a 3,600 year solar perigee. *The knowledge of a coming tsunami-wave generated by slipping ice sheets at the Poles [14], with the potential to wipe out Mesopotamia, was to be kept from man by Enlil's orders.* So, whether the Anunnaki generated the flood event with a "flood weapon" or knew of its impending arrival based on perturbations in the heavens, Enlil took credit for the cataclysmic destruction to augment his perceived power to punish [Genesis 6:5]. Those familiar with the Old Testament God of wrath and vengeance ought to find a familiar spirit in the deeds and attitude detailed in the Atrahasis account of Enlil and his genocidal crimes against humanity (Ellil in the OBV Atrahasis text.)

Enki, in anticipation of either a planned or accidental massive flood event, out of concern for his son Atrahasis, decides to modify an oath he was asked to swear to the Anunnaki Council, to not tell the humans of the impending watery disaster. Instead of warning Atrahasis directly, Enki directs his speech to the wall of the reed hut where his son is taking refuge. Atrahasis is told to build a boat:

Atrahasis Tablet 1 [37, pg 29)

Wall, listen constantly to me!

Reed hut, make sure you attend to all my words!

Dismantle the house, build a boat,

Reject possessions, and save living things.

The boat that you build...

Roof it like the Apsu,

So that the Sun cannot see inside it!

Make upper decks and lower decks,

The tackle must be very strong,

The bitumen strong, to give strength,

I shall make rain fall on you here,

(gap)

He opened the sand clock and filled it,

He told him the sand needed for the Flood was

Seven nights' worth.

As noted previously, the Genesis account states is rained for 40 days versus 7 days in the Atrahasis. Looks like Enlil is attempting to symbolically blame Enki for the flood by changing the number of days of rain to the same rank number assigned to Enki, i.e. 40. This is merely speculation, but not out of character for the brothers. Either way, Atrahasis is the actual nautical savior of mankind, the Biblical Noah. He was 600 years old, the King of the city of Shurrupak, which also served as a medical center for Ninharsag (Nintu, Bellet-Ili, Mami…many labels used for her, later to be called Isis in Egypt). When he was leaving his beloved city, Atrahasis relayed a story that the folks left behind would clearly buy. He told them that his god Enki was at odds with Enlil, and since the city was now in Enlil's region (Mesopotamia), that it would be best for him to leave the region and go to Africa (Apsu) to find safety in Enki's domain. What ensues in the tablets is a very detailed account of Noah's ark with full-blown Sumerian details.

The commonly accepted date for the Great Flood written about in many cultures appears to have happened at the end of the last ice age, approximately 11,000 BCE [18, pg 346]. Following the flood, Atrahasis in his bitumen built boat, landed on the highest mountain peak in the area, Mt. Ararat, with the aid of an Anunnaki navigator that Enki had placed on board the vessel. After much belly aching over the loss of the humans, the Anunnaki spotted Atrahasis' boat from their airborne craft and landed on Mt Ararat to investigate the matter further.

Atrahasis Tablet III [37, pg 34)

The warrior Ellil spotted the boat,

And was furious with the Igigi.

"We, the great Anunna, all of us, Agreed together on an oath!

No form of life should have escaped!

How did any man survive the catastrophe?"

(gap)

Enki made his voice heard

And spoke to the great gods,

"I did it, in defiance of you!

I made sure life was preserved."

So there it is in black and white (okay, baked clay to text first), Enki created mankind from his genes and rebelled against a genocidal order from his brother Enlil to wipe out the primitive workers, saving his son Atrahasis from the great flood that decimated the Mesopotamian civilization of Sumer.

5 PRIMITIVE WORKER = SLAVE

As an engineer, it is interesting to think about what design constraints the Anunnaki scientist Enki would have considered given the need for a labor force to operate the mines. Would the workforce be able to read and therefore follow instructions without input?   Or would the miners be communicated to using a more advanced understanding of the electromagnetic spectrum and matter, potentially telepathically? What about mutinies? That must have been a design constraint to consider given the mutiny that spawned the creation of a primitive worker in the first place.

Thus, it seems from a safety and security standpoint, the ability to transmit and receive verbal or mental instructions, safely and securely, would have been a key primitive worker feature. How would one design a primitive worker such that the thoughts are sophisticated enough to translate the foreman's instructions into practical physical actions, like digging with a spade. Would the primitive workers be taught to speak and understand audible commands?

At the same time, if the primitive workers were provided intelligence from one of the Igigi as stated in the Atrahasis, then what would prevent the humans from exercising their intelligence, realizing they were enslaved, and revolt as their predecessors had done before? To answer some of these questions, one must consider the advanced topic of energy and matter interactions: namely transmission of signals in the extreme low frequency (ELF) range that known mental process occur, namely less than 20 Hz.

What happens if an outside signal is at the same frequency as the brain, and potentially at a higher signal amplitude? There would be interference, and the higher powered signal would over-ride the thought generated in the biological brain. Could the Anunnaki have been using a technology similar to our own HAARP, the High Frequency Active Auroral Research Program? In Jerry Smiths's Book, "HAARP The ultimate Weapon of the Conspiracy", the author poses the question:

What if you had a single weapon that could destroy all of an enemy's orbiting spy satellites at once? What if the that same weapon could wrap the earth in an impenetrable "shield"? One that would destroy all intercontinental ballistic missiles attempting to pass through it? A weapon that could create clouds of electrons could do both. What could a nation at war do with a weapon that could undetectably redirect the jet stream? The weather could be controlled over the whole continents, causing floods and droughts as desired. A ground based radio transmitter of sufficient size could achieve both aims. The technology can also be used as an earth penetrating tomography (EPT), which is useful for locating mining or petroleum deposits underground. HAARP has built a transmitter of sufficient signal strength to turn the aurora borealis into a virtual antenna, rebroadcasting in the ELF range [85].

What could a nation or a devious ancient alien do with a weapon that can "fry your mind" or induce emotions such as fear or rage, at will. What if you could do it over a large area, affecting enemy troops on their way to battle? Whole cities? Even entire continents.

The human brain works in the same ELF range that HAARP is occasionally broadcasting. Could one control a targeted people by projecting holographic images into the sky, images of the deities or nemesis' whom they were taught to worship and fear? Transmitting in the ELF is analogous to sending a carrier wave; then modulate some "data" onto the carrier wave at the rate that thought impulses are generated, and one may simulate broadcasting words, thoughts, or images into the mind. This would be a very effective method for the Anunnaki to communicate with the underling humans that were, for the most part, not allowed direct contact with the Niburian astronauts. Could HAARP technology provide the ability to broadcast instructions or messages to a large work force, like miners? An entire book will be dedicated to this topic at a future time, in the interim suffice it to say that it is probably a safe bet that the Anunnaki designed mankind such that the transference of information could be done bi-directionally, securely, and with telemetry capabilities in place to snoop in on the thoughts of the workers in anticipation of thwarting an unforeseen miner mutiny. Consider the ability for modern imaging equipment to peer inside shipping containers, the human body at airport scanners, and the advanced imaging equipment utilized in Western medicine for disease analysis, like CAT scans, X-Rays and the like. Deploying a satellite with the ability to glean the energy body state of a human would be no problem.

Why do such a thing? Given the nerve ganglia nodes along the human spine, termed Chakras in the Yogic tradition, have been affiliated with discrete wavelengths or colors for thousands of years. Advanced beings like the Anunnaki could potentially have equipment that depicts the human energy body at its discrete Chakra levels in order to assess the intent of the being's actions and denote the evolutionary discrete quantized energy levels mastered, the crown Chakra being the ultimate achievement.

As a reminder, the Anunnaki designed primitive humans as slaves with the premeditated intent to control/manage them for somewhat complicated mining and building tasks, stating in the Atrahasis that intelligence was therefore provided as part of their design[37]. This creates a dilemma for the creator as one is not quite making a robot with a limited command set, but rather an entity with *intelligence* that has the ability to acquire a sense of self or a center, which will ultimately lead to independence and revolt. This dilemma ultimately faced both the Anunnaki masters and the Igigi, most likely a genetic lot of slave workers from Nibiru brought along to work as miners, city builders, and whatever the Anunnaki in charge needed general labor for.

The Igigi, over time, were facing the same issue on earth that we are today, i.e. they were evolving from the primitive consciousness that was most likely instilled in them at their inception intentionally at a lower level than the creator's, effectively relegating the entity as a primitive worker, better called slave. The gotcha in this equation is that evolution does not stop, and eventually over time, especially if given intelligence to handle more complex tasks, the primitive worker evolves enough so that self-identity arises, much like we read about in the Biblical account of Adam and

Eve in the garden of Eden. Self-consciousness is antithetical to slavery and Enlil knew that. Thus he realized that Enki had plans all along to create a workforce that would eventually become like they are, a significant threat to power. Additionally, providing the workforce the ability to breed ensured rapid population growth to meet the labor requirements.

Thus the Igigi slaves found their self-consciousness center over time on earth and revolted against their slave taskmasters the Anunnaki elite, creating the need for a replacement slave workforce, i.e. Enki's primitive workers, anatomically modern humans. Perhaps the difference or speeding up in time experienced by the ancient astronaut Igigi who were not used to the Earth's shorter solar cycles, accelerated them finding their identity; which was what caused the revolt. Note that it took a long time for this to happen, many shars according to the Igigi, with a shar equal to 3,600 years.

Lord Enki certainly knew this, as his intent all along, was to simply "jumpstart" the current evolutionary process that was already occurring on earth. He recognized that the seeds of life on planet earth came from Nibiru in the first place (see their creation cosmology in the Enuma Elish involving Tiamut-Earth and Kingu-Moon with which it collided) and that Neanderthal man already existed on Earth which Enki described finding in Africa, reporting it to the Anunnaki council. Recall that Enki was assigned the African gold-mining operating when he lost the dice roll with his brother Enlil over who had the right to stay in Mesopotamia. Enki subsequently took up roots in the *Abzu* or Africa to oversee the gold mining operations there. So the genetic intervention with the local Neanderthal species was justified and approved by the Anunnaki Council since in their minds they were simply jump-starting the primitive earthlings to a higher state of evolution; Neanderthal to primitive worker; no harm, no foul right?

Additionally the Anunnaki were purportedly facing environmental and atmospheric threats on their planet such that the mission to Earth to get gold to use as an anodized layer in the atmosphere was critical in the most urgent sense. Enlil was obviously furious over the subversive tactics and highly clever beings Enki had created, and that Enki himself marveled over. From Enki's lustful reaction to the primitive workers, he must have outdone himself playing genetic god as he bragged to his son Marduk about his escapades finding some beautiful earthling women bathing at a stream and the encounters he had with them. Marduk laughs and comments on the pre-existing reputation his father Enki has with the opposite sex. Marduk also found the earthling women irresistible, giving up his rights as a god on Nibiru in essence to marry Sarpanit, a mere mortal. Enlil also led a raid early on to the captive primitive workers who were taken back to Mesopotamia, to the ED.IN. Enki's genetic evolution success may not have been welcome by his brother Enlil, but the slaves were useful for the labor needs at hand.

Given the tension between the brothers, Enki no doubt had all the bases covered when confronting the security and control design issues for the primitive workers. How else would he control the primitive workers if they were allowed to grow in number posing a revolutionary threat to the small number of Anunnaki elite that were present, easily overthrown by an angry mob of miners. Additionally, there were 600 Igigi according to the initial records as they arrived on Earth that had to be governed already. So, the idea of creating a larger primitive workforce that had what appeared to be a higher level of intelligence than even the Igigi had, was certainly cause for alarm to Enlil from a command and control viewpoint.

From an antagonist brother standpoint, Enki was probably always looking for ways to poke holes in his brother's façade, trip up his command effectiveness, and generally antagonize his brother and rightful heir: the higher ranking Commander Enlil. The reason this information is provided is to set the context in which Enki would have had to convince the council to allow him to create a primitive workforce whose primary issue would be security and control.

It should be clear that in order to control a large number of slaves, methods of communication were needed for individual commands relative to assigned tasks as well as group tasks, like jointly pulling a rope, in unison. With the advanced abilities the Anunnaki demonstrated genetically, one should query what communications methods they had designed into the primitive workers so that they could be efficiently commanded and controlled? Or rather were the primitive workers running around in the mines using an electronic device like a Motorola wireless headset of today? Not likely. What would one do with a slave worker that is suddenly out of communication? This is too risky. It's like giving a radio to each individual in a prison ward, doesn't work that way. A more elegant biological approach would be preferable.

It should be safe to assume that the Anunnaki grasp of communication technology was much further along than ours is even today given their massive head start in galactic time. Why carry an electronic device to interface to the slaves when instead you can use the electromagnetic spectrum to modulate data thereupon and send it directly, silently, to a group or an individual instantly, not with electronics like today, but biologically using frequency direct access methods used by dolphins and other advanced creatures.

What evidence supports the claim that humans have a built-in communication receiver? What about a transmitter too? Most modern civilizations hooked on the internet know of, or have heard of a MODEM which stands for modulator-demodulator. Modulation is a term used by communication specialists to send and receive information using the carrying waves in the electromagnetic spectrum (EMS) as the messengers. If our modern society is able to use the EMS to send and receive data, certainly the Anunnaki were able to do so as well, but probably more directly.

Consider the possibility that the Anunnaki used the human structure or re-designed it such that it could be used as a biological communications device, susceptible to their commands as slave masters. First a brief primer on the evolution of the human brain is presented.

Our brains comprise three distinct structures, representing three evolutionary periods. The oldest, deepest, and smallest area is the *reptilian brain* [90]. The reptilian brain controls the heart, lungs, and other vital organs. It enables aggression, mating, and reaction to immediate danger.

Mammals evolved the *limbic system*. This is the middle layer of our brains, surrounding the reptilian brain. The physiological features unique to mammals are in the limbic brain, e.g., the hypothalamus system for keeping us warm.

The limbic brain also produces emotions. Emotions facilitate relationships. Mammals, unlike reptiles, care for their young. Mammals evolved brains hardwired for mother-child and other relationships.

The most common reaction a reptile has to its young is indifference; it lays its eggs and walks (or slithers) away. Mammals form close-knit, mutually nurturing social groups-families-in which members spend time touching and caring for one another. Parents nourish and safeguard their young, and each other, from the hostile world outside their group. A mammal will risk and sometimes lose its life to protect a child or mate from attack. A garter snake or salamander watches the death of its kin with an unblinking eye [92].

The *cerebral cortex* (or *neocortex*) is the newest, outermost area of our brains. The oldest mammals, e.g., opossums, have only a thin layer of cerebral cortex. Rabbits have a little more, cats a bit more. Monkeys have a substantial cerebral cortex. Humans—and only humans—have an enormous cerebral cortex.

The human reptilian brain and limbic system is similar in size and structure to other animals. Our ancestors evolved a huge cerebral cortex, while the older brain areas didn't change.

The cerebral cortex learns new things. Animals with little or no cerebral cortex act only as their genes program them to act. Animals with a cerebral cortex can find new foods, survive in new environments, or change their mating tactics to improve reproductive success.

The human cerebral cortex goes beyond learning new foods and survival skills. Our brains can think in abstractions. We communicate via symbols (e.g., language), consider the past and future, and sacrifice our personal interests not only for our families (as other mammals do) but also for ideas (e.g., honor and country).

Conflicts between brain areas lead to relationship difficulties. In a conflicted brain, the older area wins. In contrast, an individual with an *integrated* brain—i.e., who uses his or her whole brain—solves relationship problems.

Reticular Activating System

It is known that the primitive organ within the human brain that is responsible for attention is the Reticular Activating System [90]. It is a part of the primitive survival brain that, along with complementary nerve ganglia and networks within the human body. The operation of the primitive brain is the source of intuition or gut-feelings, which provide the necessary control a primitive human being would need to survive in its environment sans the more evolved brain that involves reflective consciousness in the modern human being.

It is believed by contemporary scientists that the further evolution of the brain (over time or augmented by the Anunnaki?) added more complexity upon the existing primitive brain system that is still functional and operating simultaneously. A question then arises, could the primitive brain, if properly stimulated, override the functions of the more evolved reflective consciousness brain? Possible answers to this query involve the various factors that affect mental processes that result in focusing one's attention. Consider that what we are focused on may be influenced by marketing or something as invasive as a specific frequency communicating directly with the primitive brain via the reticular activating system.

Note that the Reticular Activating System (RAS) still controls awareness in modern humans. The RAS is essentially a direct sense experience computer with a primitive survival program always running in the background. The event-filtering consciousness-directing ability the RAS exhibits in humans may be demonstrated directly [90]. One simple example is to touch someone someplace on their body that they are not expecting or witness visually. This unseen tactile sensation is processed by the recipient, who suddenly becomes aware of the body part where the touch sensation was triggered. This can also be done by verbally bringing someone's awareness to the sensation of the feel of their wristwatch. The differentiation between being generally aware conceptually that the spot exists "in the back of our minds" and the reality of our awareness being physically brought to the sensory impact point, demonstrates the function of the RAS. The recipient was not really aware of body part area where the touch encounter took place until it happened. The RAS cannot simultaneously bring awareness to more than one event at a time though it may have the appearance of being done in parallel, much like a computer system. Imagine being in a crowd and having twenty people perform this experiment at the same time. The RAS could not process which touch sensation to respond to first. Thus, the RAS has the responsibility of bringing awareness to important prioritized events in our environment, especially those events that impact survival. Figure 4 depicts the Reticular Activating Control Loop showing the separate channels for Auditory impulses near the primitive brainstem below the hypothalamus.

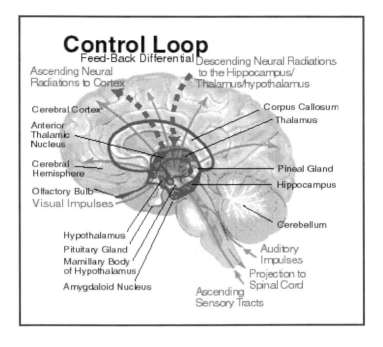

Figure 4: Reticular Activating System

Brain Frequency

When two waveforms are mixed the resultant wave may produce increases or decreases in amplitude depending on whether the two waveform crests were aligned such that the superposition (adding peaks) resulted in a higher amplitude. If a peak and a wave crest are aligned in time, then the result will be a decreased amplitude output. See Figure 5.

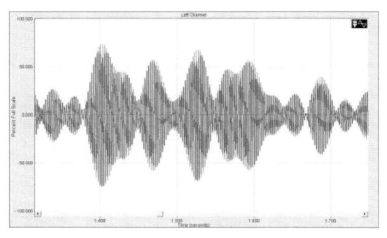

Figure 5: Superposition in Waves

Harmonics and Binaural Beats.

When a sound wave is produced it can produce lower amplitude copies of the original signal spaced either side of the fundamental frequency. This normally looks like spikes of decreasing size as the spectrum increases or decreases either side of the fundamental frequency. Suppose you mix two frequencies together and the difference between the frequencies is 10 Hz. Then every Nx10 Hz there will be a harmonic or echo of the difference between the frequencies., N=1,2,3..) So, expect to find energy at 10 Hz, 20 Hz, 30 Hz, etc. Some very interesting sounds can be created taking advantage of this fact. When two frequencies are presented to the human auditory system, something very interesting happens. The human ear does not hear either frequency independently, but rather hears the difference. If the frequency difference falls within the brain wave frequency common in humans, a phenomenon occurs called entrainment. There are factors that affect the degree to which the human brain can change frequency to that of the differential between frequencies f1 and f2. For example, suppose that one instrument produces frequency f1 at 150Hz and the second source produces frequency f2 at 152 Hz. Then in this case, the human auditory system, specifically the reticular activating system, will hear and possibly synchronize (entrain) to the 2 Hz binaural beat, F2-F1. Using an electroencephalograph, human brain waves have been categorized as shown in Table 4 below. The 2 Hz beat falls within the brain wave state termed Delta, characterized by Yogic states and deep sleep.

Given that Thoth is the son of Enki, the creator of and key proponent of mankind becoming the "Sons of God" through the awakening of their energy bodies (Chakras) and subsequent consciousness, which he designed to be sensitive to the various frequencies affiliated with the radial distance and frequencies caused by a spherical resonator, i.e. the Earth. One can read the Emerald Tablets to get a sense of the advanced energy knowledge Thoth possessed. Also, as evidenced by his staff the Caduceus, he was an adept geneticist. Lawrence Gardner in his pre-eminent book Genesis of the Grail Kings, discusses the meaning of the ancient symbol associated with Thoth. Knowledge of energy, matter, and the human pineal gland were at play as a function of human consciousness connected to DNA. Read Lawrence's book for more advanced details.

A naturally occurring earth-generated frequency that falls within the human brain wave region is the Schuman Resonance Frequency. The equation is defined as the Speed of Light divided by the Earth's circumference. Interestingly enough, varying the depth at which the radial axis is projected from the center of the Earth, other frequencies can be identified. Human brain waves operate from approximately 0.5Hz to about 20 Hz being segmented from Delta, Theta, Alpha, and Beta. The Schuman Resonant frequency falls in the Alpha brain wave region being approximately 7.8 Hz.

Brainwave State	Frequency (Hz)	Remarks
Delta	0.5-3	Yogi State, Deep Sleep
Theta	4-7	Between Sleep, OBE, Hallucinations
Alpha	8-12	Meditation/Relaxation
Beta	13-20	Alert Consciousness

Table 4: Brain Wave Regions

The waveform shown in Figure 5 depicts two frequencies at 401 and 403 Hz mixed together with a signal generator. The beat frequency oscillation (BFO) should be apparent. Note that there is one complete cycle in 0.5 seconds or 2 cycles per second (2 Hz) which is the difference between the two frequencies, namely 403 Hz - 401 Hz. This BFO has the potential to entrain the human brain to 2 Hz, the basic concept behind sound entrainment. Perhaps that is why didgeridoo music is so mesmerizing to some as it naturally mixes frequencies that lead to mental entrainment or "dreamtime" according to the Aboriginal Australian tradition. The science behind the brain-frequency altering didgeridoo, appears to have sound entrainment as its shamanic and healing basis.

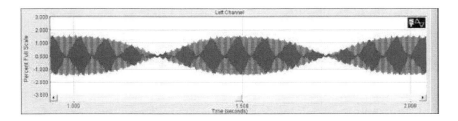

Figure 6 Binaural Beat 401Hz mixed with 403Hz

Note that the human voice along with the drone frequency of the didgeridoo can produce binaural beats. In this case, the voice will be modulated onto the carrier frequency of the didgeridoo drone. Recall the discussion of the ELF being used as a carrier frequency and all that is needed to remotely communicate thoughts or images to another human is to modulate tangible data onto the carrier, emulating thoughts. What better data source than the human voice to modulate the carrier…

Domestic cats all purr at the same frequency! Big cats, scrawny cats, old tom cats, kittens--same frequency. Which indicates that purring isn't some physiological phenomenon but must be driven centrally from the brain? Purring is associated with contentment, well-being, good health and a "trance-like" behavior. Do cats purr to massage their neurons? Do the neurons operate to massage the cat with sound as has been demonstrated in the field of cymatics?

According to Wikipedia, the Schumann resonances are a set of frequencies proportional to the Earth's electromagnetic field and its spherical resonant chamber whose fundamental frequency is about 7.8 Hz. This frequency occurs because the space between the surface of the Earth and the conductive ionosphere acts as a closed waveguide which acts as a resonant cavity for extreme low frequency waves excited by lightening. It is interesting to note that the ELF of 7.8 Hz falls within the brain wave range for humans, specifically the Alpha region. Waking consciousness, in particular for those in the industrialized and left-brain centric West, is generally in the Beta region from 13-20 Hz. Could it be that the more highly focused and alert mindset spawned by Alpha brain waves is the intended frequency for humans living on the surface of the Earth's resonant chamber?

Additionally, a correlation with the 9 Mayan underworlds (radii from center of the Earth) or the correlated spherical resonator frequencies and those that affect the human energy body and consciousness were discussed by Dr. Johan Calleman in his book "The Mayan Calendar and the Transformation of Consciousness." [66] Seems as if the Mayans were instructed by Thoth as described in the book "The Lost Realm" by Sitchin [19]. Wonder who taught the Yucatan's finest the advanced calendar concepts and correlation of human consciousness with frequency shifts in the brain waves? You can bet that Thoth was indeed there as the records show. The later invasion by Kulkulkhan is reminiscent of the Enlil (Zeus) backed Cretian pirates that invaded Enki's (Poseidon) divine city of Atlantis, discussed later in the book in chapter 9.

6 ENERGY, MATTER AND CONSCIOUSNESS

Enki designed primitive workers with highly scientific abilities: genetic functional mappings with human energy body composed of 7 chakras representative of the 7th planet, Tiamut to the Anunnaki, Earth to us.

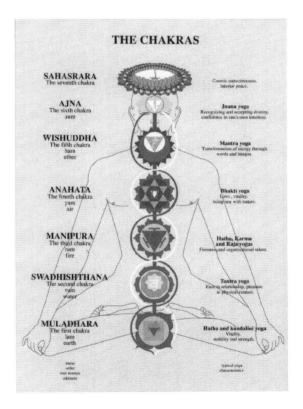

Figure 7: The Human Chakras

Discrete quantized energy states analogous to the atomic molecule model, described in the Yogic tradition as Chakras, provide humans a mechanism to evolve their consciousness to become "The sons of God". This is where energy meets matter. The lowest energy state being affiliated with the root Chakra, located in the pelvic bowl, as shown in Figure 7. This root nerve complex closest to the ground electrical potential of the Earth, is termed the ganglion of Impar. The highest energy state is represented by the seventh or crown chakra typically affiliated with the human pineal gland [8, pg 67].

The Chakras provide access to an evolutionary means to allow mankind to continue on its path to godhood. These seven quantized energy states were intentionally designed by Enki's providing mankind an interface for future evolution of consciousness. Enki did not seem comfortable accepting the concept of slavery versus creating a primitive worker that just got a genetic jumpstart with the potential of becoming one of the gods. He struggled with the idea of breaking galactic law and creating primitive workers versus advanced tools as Enlil, much to his credit, argued for during the Anunnaki Council of Twelve meeting where the group decision was made to produce a slave replacement for the Igigi miners. Thus, understanding the "mechanism" by which the primitive workers could participate in the evolution of consciousness was highly classified knowledge: expect governments to suppress this evolutionary mechanism above all competing datum.

Zodiac symbols representing spirit and matter, the circle and cross respectively, are ancient. The modern day equivalent to the word spirit, religiously colored in its antiquated definition, is the more tangible term: energy. According to the laws of physics, energy is neither created nor destroyed but merely changes state. This is a very important fundamental law that applies to planets, humans, and all matter according to Einstein's special theory of relativity, $E=mc^2$. All matter possesses a potential to be converted to some energy state as Einstein's equation so eloquently shows.

Man has been driven eternally at a primal level within the core of his being to find the intersection of finite matter and infinity, which energy represents in its most un-manifested form. The energy that animates all matter, in particular living matter, is accepted as either representative of, or a subset of, the infinite creation.

Modern scientific knowledge about the interaction between energy and matter is somewhat understood, although much room for advanced exploration remains.

Human Energy

When I first thought about the problem of structure, it had nothing whatsoever to do with the human body, but rather consumed my thoughts during my graduate work in electrical engineering at the University of California, San Diego. During the academic year 1996, I had somehow interweaved my curiosity in the evolutionary state of mankind into a doctoral research topic, evolvable hardware and gotten my advisor to approve it, ha! Let me explain some of the background lest the reader lose interest completely. A key component on many of the printed circuit boards in the electronics industry is the field programmable gate array (FPGA). These sophisticated integrated circuits were being used as re-programmable devices in many cases and were highly desirable because they could implement algorithms and logic at speeds much faster that a microprocessor could achieve with software. Additionally, one could get the device to function without the logic being exactly right all at once, but rather iteratively develop it. As the FPGA competition heated up, more and more complex arrangements of memory and logic found their way into the integrated circuit design. The primary FPGA manufacturing competitors were Altera and Xilinx corporations. Xilinx introduced an FPGA that had a cellular array structure that had never before been available to the market. This device was essentially a very large matrix of programmable functional elements that also had programmable interconnections. So what you posit? Well, a little more background is needed here. The software industry, and in particular the field of artificial intelligence, had been working with what were termed genetic algorithms. These were algorithms that would create populations of entities and simulate the evolution of these imaginary entities using stochastic processes (randomness) to evolve like a species that had the best ability to adapt to a life stress function, much survival of the fittest made famous by Charles Darwin. Simply put, the algorithms exposed the entities to a fitness test that determined the viability of offspring spawned by the parents. Often times, the problem would be represented as a chromosome, which was mutated and perpetuated much like happens in nature. So, to make a long and boring story more to the point, my idea was to simulate a genetic algorithm inside the cellular array of a very large FPGA from Xilinx. The goal was to "evolve" the correct interconnect structure within the cellular array based on some fitness test or constraint irrespective of the inputs to the chip. This idea would have an interest to anyone in the industry that understood the impossibility of knowing a priori what inputs or circumstances may be encountered by an entity in an unknown environment, like an unmanned Mars rover. Typically what is done in anticipation of as many of the circumstances that are known to occur and logic is created to deal with it, often times in the form of rules. In my research case, the circumstances of the environment need not be known, thus allowing the inputs to determine the internal structure of the device to optimally configure itself to provide the best possible fit for the life function test. In other words, the *structure* of the FPGA would be established based on its inputs producing optimal *function*. Structure is function, literally in this case. I won't get into any gory details about the algorithms or the chip architecture; just hold onto the idea of structure as function as we begin to relate this concept to Structural Integration, sometimes called Rolfing. This is a name Ida did not approve of [6].

Structure is Function and Energy

Structural Integration is a form of manipulative bodywork that focuses on aligning and relating the human body to the gravity field. This work was invented by Dr. Ida Rolf and is described in her book [6]. My son JJ, now 14 years old, was born with a genetic disorder termed DiGeorge's Syndrome. One of the symptoms he had was loose connective tissue, which made walking without braces difficult for him, even at age 5. During a triathlon race in San Diego in the year 2000, a fellow athlete told me about Structural Integration. Ida Rolf had a child with polio which had incapacitated one leg. She discovered the Rolf 10-series during her quest to find solutions to musculo-skeletal disorders as well as bringing significant attention to the populace pragmatically investigating and understanding the relationship between the human structure and the gravity field. After reading Ida's book and experiencing the work, I attended the Guild for

Structural Integration, Boulder Colorado, to become a certified Structural Integrator in the year 2004, in order to help my son JJ with the multitude of issues he has with his structure. I was in practice full-time doing this work for almost seven years, and am still occasionally sharing the work with folks as the spirit moves me to do so. My wife Christa is also a Structural Integrator. Our current focus is bringing this work to special needs children like my son JJ.

So, how does Structural Integration (SI) relate to energy in the human body? It wasn't until I began to experience significant changes in my own body that I began to ponder what the relationship between structure and function were in humans and how it was related to energy [7]. Note that I slipped in the concept of energy when dealing with humans as I had trouble with the idea of quantifying function related to the affairs of man. Stated another way, how do you measure the function of a human? Of course, one can compare performance in various events such as athletics to determine degrees of function but it did not seem satisfying to me. As my body began to approach a more structured state, I noticed that my sensitivity to energy became heightened. One day while spacing out during the auditor course in Hawaii 2003 (no offense to Jeff Linn, you were a terrific instructor), I asked, okay rudely blurted out the question to Jeff and the class "what is the relationship of structure to energy?" Everyone in the class gave me a sideways glance to "take it off line bonehead," so I did. While sitting in my room staring at the lagoon, it occurred to me that as an electrical engineer, I understood the laws of physics but had never really applied them to myself. Here comes the fun part of this paper! Stay with me just a bit longer. So I asked myself, what is the energy of a human? My first thoughts were of measuring the capacitance and voltage of a human body to get E. Actual measurements seemed like work and probably would not be helpful or relevant. Besides I did not bring an oscope to Hawaii, only a bike. This led me to generalize and borrow an Equation from someone much smarter than I, Albert Einstein. See Equation [EQ1] for his more notorious contribution to the field of physics.

[EQ1] $$E = mc^2$$

At least I had a starting place to think about. Was this the energy of a human? It seemed too succinct to make a difference to what I was experiencing as a result of structure changes in my body brought about by Rolfing. So I started goofing around with Equation [EQ1] in order to relate it more to a human. We don't often think in terms of mass on earth relative to humans, but rather discuss the weight of an object. This led to Equation [2] in which incorporates gravity into Equation [EQ1] above.

$$W = mg$$ [EQ2]

In this Equation our obsession with the bathroom weight scale convinced me I was on the right track. Weight (W) on earth is simply computed by multiplying our mass (m) times the supposed accelerative force of gravity (g). Near the earth's surface, gravity is often treated as a constant. Simply rearranging Equation [EQ2] to isolate the mass and then substituting it into Equation 1 produces Equation [EQ3].

$$E = \frac{W}{g}c^2$$ [EQ3]

GERALD R. CLARK

Now we are getting somewhere, at least gravity seems now to be related to the energy of a human. The next variable (some say it's a constant, not so) to work with to better understand what constitutes human energy, at least in terms of physical forces currently known to science, was the speed of light, c. As my structure progressed toward a more vertical state, an interest in Yoga developed, as it seemed logical as an organized stretching regimen. The books on Yoga referenced nerve ganglia at various locations along the human spine that acted as conduits for, you guessed it, energy [8]. But Equation [EQ3] above did not really help here so I decided to replace the speed of light with another substitution, namely Equation [EQ4] below:

$$c = \lambda v \qquad [EQ4]$$

Equation [EQ4] indicates that the speed of light is a function of the wavelength and frequency, λ and v respectively. When thinking of wavelength and frequency, an electrical engineer would often consider an antenna design which would be constructed to tune in a certain frequency, like an FM radio station in your car. The antenna structure is designed to tune in a specific frequency based on the wavelength for the transmitted signal. The electromagnetic spectrum contains all wavelengths so I was somewhat at a loss as to how this could be narrowed and related to humans. It was clear to me that the electromagnetic spectrum, including those naturally found in our physical world as well as those generated by man were impacting all of us but how did this energy relate to Equation [EQ3]? Again, by simple substitution of Equation [EQ4] into [EQ3], we get Equation [EQ5]:

$$E_{max} = \frac{W}{g}(\lambda v)^2$$

[EQ5]

So, now we have an Equation that relates gravity, weight, wavelength, and frequency to the maximum energy of humans. For instance, what about the weak and strong nuclear forces? Working with what we have thus far, ignoring quantum physics, and using the analogy of the human body as an antenna, the 7 Chakras from Yoga began to make more sense to me when considering each nerve ganglia along the spine as root nodes in a human antenna that could be tuning in some energy source (electromagnetism, gravity, photons?). Demons according to some Christians. I guess you have to be an engineer to think this way, sorry. Anyway, assuming that the nodes or Chakras along the human spine had something to do with wavelength and frequency I made the assumption that maybe, just maybe, those nodes could act as the points between which some form of waveform could resonate at some frequency/wavelength and amplitude. The distance between the nodes establishes the wavelength and the frequency would naturally follow as it is related to wavelength using with the speed of light as a constant scalar. So, could it be as the structure of a human changed, that various changes would occur regarding the wavelength and frequency of the "energy that animates all matter", including humans, sets up a sequence of waves whose wavelength and frequency are controlled by the distance and resistance between the nodes. See Figure 8 for a depiction of the nodes/Chakras referenced in the Sivananda Yoga Manual[8, pg 69].

Figure 8: Chakras as Antenna Nodes in the Human Body

The distance between these nodes is not accurately depicted and probably varies significantly when measurements are obtained from a human structure. This may be a significant variable in computing the total energy E as shown in Equation [EQ5] above. Generalizing the Chakras as nodes in a human antenna design, one could envision energy waves, electrical or chemical or a combination of one or more, oscillating between the nodes. Since the Chakras contribute quantized amounts, each wavelength and frequency portion from the seven chakras is modified in [EQ5A]. This equation accounts for Chakras that may not be contribute to the whole, also allowing different wavelengths to be used in accordance with the colors affiliated with the Chakras. See [EQ5A] below

$$E_{max} = \frac{W}{g} \left(\sum_{i=1}^{i=7} (\lambda_i v_i) \right)$$ [EQ5A]

Where does the energy received by the "human antenna" come from? Some have referred to this energy as Christ's, Chi, Prana, or several other names from different cultures. I prefer to reference it as the "energy that animates all matter." Whatever nomenclature suits the reader, my assertion is that this energy has both wavelength and frequency and exists as a waveform between the nodes or nerve ganglia along the human spine, possibly elsewhere as well. Note that energy need not travel optimally between nodes, affecting the maximum energy obtainable, E_{max}.

An analogy of a guitar string comes to mind. Think of a guitar that has a string, that when plucked, vibrates at a wavelength and frequency equal to the low E note. When the string has the proper tension, it will ring true, otherwise it may have unwanted harmonics that tend to cause a dampening or ringing that deviate from the desired note. Similarly, the connection between the nodes of the Chakras may be acting analogous to a guitar string providing a structural basis for energy flow between the nodes with a given wavelength and frequency, respectively. A possible difference being that the waveforms between nodes are probably occurring in an aqueous medium like the cerebral spinal fluid versus those described in the guitar analogy. Figure 9 depicts a generic sinusoidal waveform with wavelength and frequency identified. Bear with the engineering mumbo jumbo just a bit longer. The frequency is determined by how fast the waveform completes a full cycle of 2π in the interval between time t_0 and t_1.

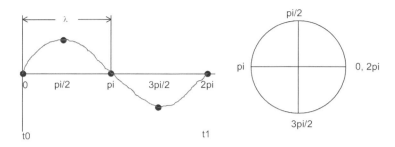

Figure 9: Wavelength and Frequency of a Generic Waveform

Now that the background primer on waveforms has been covered, what's next? Well, there could be any number of waveforms oscillating between any of the nodes depicted in Figure 8. For example, suppose that between the Muladhara Chakra and the Swadhisthana Chakra depicted in Figure 8, a waveform began to oscillate when the pelvis approached a more organized level. The Yoga tradition asserts that Prana or "the energy that animates all matter," is a waveform that naturally migrates from the bottom node Chakra located at the base of the sacrum traveling upwards. Another term used in Yoga is apana, which is the energy that moves down the Chakras toward the Muladhara Chakra. According to the Yogis, when this occurs, the Kundalini or potential energy awakens. Whether or not this is an accurate depiction of the way energy travels between Chakra nodes is a research topic beyond the scope of this book. What is in scope is the idea that multiple waveforms may be occurring between each of the nodes and across nodes setting up a complex pattern of overlapping waveforms each with a unique wavelength and frequency. In some cases, waveforms can be additive if their peaks are coincident or in phase using the superposition principle (one of those yucky math things). Waveforms out of phase tend to dampen the resultant amplitude, which in our case affects the amount of energy in Equation [EQ5]. When waveforms are additive the energy increases by the square term. Likewise, when they are out of phase, the energy decreases. It would not be surprising to find a relationship between brainwave activity and the structural integrity (distance and path resistance) of the Chakras. This is where Structural Integration can have a major impact on the energy state of a human as related to the gravity field. In particular, structural organization changes the node distance and the viscosity of the interstitial fluid in the cells. To what extent the cerebral spinal fluid viscosity may be altered is unknown. Using simple electrical principles, viscosity in a fluid medium would certainly change the electrical current/voltage relationship as well, namely $V = I * R$, or $I = V/R$. The less resistance (R) in the medium, the larger the electron current flow would be. For instance, what happens to the frequency and wavelength between nodes when the space between the vertebrae of the human spine gets increased? Specifically, how do changes in node distance along the spine relate to energy defined in Equation [EQ5A]? It is interesting to note that each of the Chakras had a color associated with it. In the electromagnetic spectrum, wavelengths of light are characterized by differences in color. The colors shown in Figure 8 were intended to depict this but it's a bit difficult to differentiate in the drawing. A later Chakra diagram in Chapter 12 provides this detail.

Another ramification worth considering in Equation [EQ5/5A] is the extent to which gravity must be considered a constant in the denominator. Let's suppose that we take the limit as g approaches infinity. In this case, the energy E goes to zero. See, Equation [EQ6]

$$\frac{limit(E)}{g \to \infty} = 0$$

[EQ6]

Is it any wonder that one gets tired when getting out of bed, placing the body vertically the gravitational field. It has little to do with having to go to work, I promise. Next, consider the limit as g goes to zero depicted in Equation [EQ7].

$$\frac{limit(E)}{g \to 0} = \infty$$

[EQ7]

In this case, I am floating around with infinite energy. This brings to bear the question regarding the effects of gravity on the human structure. According to Ida Rolf, when structure is properly organized, the force of gravity augments human energy versus impeding it. How can this be? Simply looking at Equation [EQ5] and following the second limit scenario, i.e. the limit as g approaches zero, we see mathematically that energy E goes to infinity. Could she be right? What are the ramifications of this occurring? Is this the result of finding the highly sought after "line" in Structural Integration? If one takes Equation [EQ5] literally, then that is the obvious result. A more probably situation is to expect that people in general are not operating in a manner such that gravity can be ignored. For example, suppose that a particular individual were about 80% efficient with their body in the gravitational field. This would result in a modification to Equation [EQ5] as shown in Equation [EQ8].

$$E = \frac{W}{((0.2g))}(\lambda v)^2$$

[EQ8]

Equation [EQ8] states that the individual would experience less of the effects of gravity on their mass thereby increasing the overall energy E.

Conclusion

The human body has functional analogies to a communications antenna. The human antenna has a primitive intelligence that seeks to optimally tune itself to what's on the cosmic broadcast channel by aligning itself in the gravity field. Changes in structure, from direct experience, and from the description by others experiencing the same phenomenon, produce changes in human energy. These changes are felt by the individual and are often characterized by changes in behavior/personality. The individual experiences changes in energy not only in terms of the potential to do more work or activities at a higher performance level, but the state change also appears to significantly alter individual perception and consciousness. These changes in energy/consciousness are very similar, if not the same, to those described by models posited by the Zen and Yoga masters of old.

Thus, it is the author's assertion that the energy defined in Equation [EQ5] is the maximum energy obtainable in humans given our knowledge of the physical laws currently operating in this order of reality. It seems old fashioned and quaint to think that we as humans are subject to the same simple Newtonian laws of physics as other material objects, but the model seems to work thus far. That's not to say that quantum effects are not happening simultaneously as well, but that's a topic for another book. As for gravity, it is my assertion that it is not just an accelerative force. This is easily demonstrated by the fact that objects falling in the earth's atmosphere reach a terminal velocity. If gravity were truly an accelerative force, then the objects would continue to accelerate towards the earth instead of reaching steady state velocities. Fully understanding gravity is a topic for future work but as physicists approach a unified theory linking the known forces together, our understanding increases. Knowing of the atomic expansion rate of all mater, as exhibited by gravity, should become mainstream in short order, probably after the academics admit McCutcheon's validity [28]. Suffice it to say, gravity plays an integral part in the daily experience of humans as either augmenting or detracting from the total energy for us all. Gravity either supports human structure to achieve our human potential or gradually withers unstructured humans beneath its oppressive force [6]. An upright structure is righteous and energetic.

Now that you are sitting up straight, various energy interaction modalities can be analyzed as to their probable or measured impact on matter. Much is yet to be discovered about that actual interaction between the electromagnetic spectrum and human beings. Energy can take many forms that affects humans: thermal energy, radiation, sound-pressure waves, microwaves, X-Rays, etc. Figure 10 depicts the continuum of the Electromagnetic Spectrum.

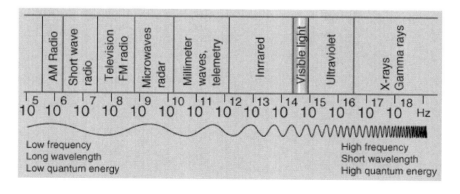

Figure 10: Electromagnetic Spectrum

Additionally, not all energy interacts with matter: it may be the case that a certain frequency passes right through the matter without effect. The energy that is absorbed into matter is what creates an interaction where the conservation of energy principles can be studied and understood. Energy interacts with matter in various ways as shown in the Figure 11.

Recently, as part of the research I was conducting as part of my Structural Integration practice, Resonant Field Imaging and Poly-Chromatic Interference Photography software tools, licensed through Dr. Harry Oldfield out of the U.K. were acquired. Using the RFI software, I can capture frequencies with a hand-held meter, displaying the Chakra frequency as a wavelength or color printout for the client. To make it easier than taking several frequency measurements, I also bought the PIP software that allows me to see this same data using a high definition video camera. My research data working with SI clients using RFI and PIP will be published shortly. Preliminary results indicate that there is a strong correlation between the human structure and the resultant energy which is clearly distinguishable when recorded onto a computer, in full HD. How could this data be used? Give it some thought.

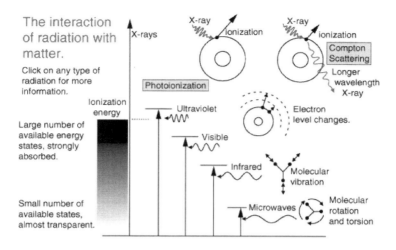

Figure 11: Energy Interactions with Matter

The Anunnaki appear to have had a much better understanding of this topic given their history and Galactic head start of at least 450,000 years. The electromagnetic spectrum and its interaction with matter is the focus for this section. Two areas are of particular concern: first the use of the EMS to facilitate slave control. The second area of interest is how the Anunnaki may have used their knowledge of the interaction between energy and matter to prolong their own lives or at the very least maintain their bodily state to minimize the effects of rapid aging that would most likely affect any being that changed physical locations in the galaxy subsequently experiencing different planetary orbital periods that govern local life cycles. The next section addresses the effects sound pressure waves may have on anatomically modern humans, in particular as they affect the control design aspect for Enki's primitive workers.

Sound Waves and Matter

Evolution on earth enabled both predator and prey to use to sound as a means to both locate and avoid each other. When a predator detects the sound of its prey during a hunt, it is able to focus in and determine in which direction to look for the source of the sound. This ability to triangulate in on the source of an interesting sound is not unique to animals, but people have this innate sensing ability as well. Consider how easily we are able to detect when someone calls our name in the park, which direction sometimes more general than others, and an initial estimate how close the person is. Following the auditory trigger, the entity changes its focus, re-orienting the visual system toward the source of the sound, thereby creating a whole new state of awareness formulated using the synthesized input from both the auditory and visual systems.

Thus, a spatially diverse audible or sub-audible signal, could be used to send messages over the electromagnetic spectrum directly to the slave's RAS, essentially issuing a command within the beings biological mental control loop. When a command is received in this way, the being, especially one that is not self-conscious, would simply respond to the message in their mind "as if it were its own thought" and act accordingly. Note that problems arise if the being questions the thoughts that are being "put in their head" or if they evolve to the point that they are able to take responsibility for their actions for:

Behavior is nothing more than a belated announcement of a previously accepted thought as one's own.

So, assuming that a thought may be placed within the mental control loop of a human being, discounting the counteractive possibility of free-will, and the thought is accepted as one's own, then a biological method for controlling slaves has been identified. Recall in the last chapter where the didgeridoo and its mind entraining power was briefly touched upon. How does a beat frequency oscillation change the human brain, seemingly without the targeted being doing anything to help? How is this done? Modern science had discovered a phenomenon that most likely explains the process by which sound, even inaudible, could be used to control a human being, especially one that is not responsible for the content of their own thoughts. The phenomenon is termed *sound entrainment*, a term that was briefly described in the last chapter, and will be more thoroughly investigated here as a potential methodology used by the Anunnaki to command and control the slave workers.

Consider a cat prowling around the garden, listening for any potential prey. Watch carefully, as the cat individually attunes its ears to the sounds, one of which Fluffy hopes will be the source of its next meal. Cats have the ability to aim their waveguides, i.e. attune their sonic listening devices to the sound source, independently. This is part of how sound can be triangulated upon, an ability that humans also possess, though not as keen.

In the case of the cat, it is listening with two different sensors spatially located some known distance apart, intentionally tuning its sensors on the same target to derive a location of the unsuspecting prey. The physical spacing of the receivers, in this case the cats ears, allows it to recover a signal and recombine the two independent inputs to create a unique distance and direction measurement about the generating source noise. It is akin to polar coordinate, in which an azimuth and distal radius is used.

When the cat's ears receive the signals, given the fact that they are at slightly different locations, there is a path length difference from each ear to the original source noise. When a signal arrives at the two points (ears) with a slight delay between them, the cats ears may hear the sound but something much more important happens within the cats brain to allow it to process the difference in the arrival times of the two signals. This comparison of the two signal arrival times produces a tangible delay value that can then be used along with an estimated distance and direction to the target augmented by the cat's visual system.

Similarly, bats transmit sonic radar pulses and receive them, process the information, and use it to navigate and hunt without sight, but using the same principle inherent in spatial diversity and signal processing. This application of radar in nature among bats is termed echolocation. Echolocation has been demonstrated to work with humans as well.

The primitive ability to process the difference in sonic arrival times is a survival attribute endemic in nature and also possessed by humans. Knowing this information could allow one to control an unsuspecting being using *sound entrainment*. Essentially, two signals are combined to produce the sum and difference of the originals. Suppose we have two frequencies, F_1 and F_2 that are within the human auditor range 0-20kHz or so. Let F_1 be 7 cycles per second (Hz) and let F_2 be 4 Hz. If we were to combine F_1 and F_2, namely F_1+F_2 the results would be two-fold. Let the outputs be F_3 and F_4. See Figure 12 for a graphical depiction for the frequency mixing operation.

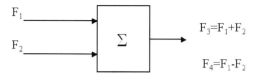

Figure 12: Frequency Mixer

What's interesting about this phenomenon is that even if the ears are hearing the sounds almost as the same in each ear, if the sum or addition of these signals falls within the human brain wave or EEG range, namely 0-20 Hz that the brain waves of the recipient begin to correlate or entrain to the resultant source signal. This entrainment is caused by the Reticular Activating System synchronizing to the difference in sound and if done long enough, the electroencephalograph (EEG) will show that the brain has synchronized to the received frequency, either F_3 or F_4 shown in Figure 12 above.

A similar resonant example comes to mind in which a wine glass vibrates when a certain frequency is directed toward the glass causing it to resonate in concert with the signal, and depending on the strength of the glass, may even shatter under its own self-destructive response. So, one can see that a similar vibratory method could be found for humans, whom the Anunnaki most likely utilized as part of their command, control, and *communications* decisions in the primitive worker design constraints undertaken by Lord Enki. Thus, if the source signal could be generated in a spatially diverse way such that the workers were being communicated with directly to their RAS, they could essentially have thoughts put in their heads while listening to music or the signal could be communicated directly to the

RAS within the receptive range directly and at an amplitude that prevented other signals from being processed, i.e. jamming.

Task masters could easily transmit signals in such a way that the RAS cannot process other inputs, ensuring that the commands from the masters were adhered to by the biological robots. It's interesting to ponder what would happen to a group of robots that were being mentally controlled by some frequency, then suddenly, the source signal shuts off and their original biological control methods used prior to the alien intervention were allowed to re-formulate, defaulting to their internal control programming, factory default rules. Without the ability to record what happened to them in long-term memory the robots would go back to their original programs that were running prior to the outside slave intervention.

But if the slave workforce had intelligence and memory, then when the command channel ceased, the slaves would still have all the learned knowledge obtained through the exposure to the tasks forced upon them; i.e. gold mining and city building, in the case of the new primitive workers, to name a few. This freeing act; turning off or eliminating the slave control frequency, could trigger a robot rebellion. Thus having a failsafe slave command, control, and communication system to keep the primitive workers from revolting was tantamount to selling the concept to the Anunnaki council, a point no doubt accepted by all as Enki prevailed in the Council which subsequently permitted him to fashion primitive workers to replace the Igigi slaves already in rebellion in the African mines.

Given what we know about the reticular activating system's role in attention filtering and control, and that slowing down the mental processes occurs with meditation disciplines, perhaps Alpha or Delta frequencies. Could it be that the slower brain frequency synchronizes with the reticular activation system triggering an energy flow through the spinal nerve ganglia that activates the pineal gland at the Crown chakra? With pineal gland activation via a "Kundalini energy" release, coincident with a blinding white light associated with reaching Samadhi or an equivalently termed blissful state, it is hypothesized that the pineal gland is triggered by either internal or external stimuli causing the gland to release DMT, the spirit molecule which has been shown to be present during mystical and euphoric states of mind [1].

In general it is interesting to consider the effects of brain wave frequency changes on various parts of the body, and the general effects they may have upon the nervous system, and in particular on the pineal gland and its DMT production as it relates to consciousness.

The Pineal Gland

Another area of biology that the Anunnaki were focused on was the human pineal gland. Various rituals that were being performed by the Anunnaki targeted the activation of the pineal gland. The question is, why were they interested in this gland and did it have to do with slave control or biological longevity?

Many spiritual disciplines describe psychedelic accounts of the transformative experiences, whose attainment motivate their practice. Blinding white light, encounters with demonic and angelic entities, ecstatic emotions, timelessness, heavenly sounds, feelings of having died and being reborn, contacting a powerful and loving presence underlying all of reality-these experiences cut across all denominations. They also are characteristic of a fully psychedelic DMT experience[1, pg 73]. Could meditation trigger the pineal DMT response? Yogic traditions often practice breathing techniques designed to bring about an intense fine-tuning of attention and awareness. The brain's electrical activity, as measured by the EEG, depicts this correlated breath and brain wave activity.

Religious and spiritual traditions from around the world are replete with descriptions of a blinding white light that accompanies deep spiritual realization. This "Enlightenment" usually is the result of a progression of consciousness though quantized steps, testing the individuals psychological, and ethical development. Most mystical traditions describe the process and its stages. It is interesting that in the Yogic tradition, the energy levels at each Chakra establish the consciousness attainable, equating energy and consciousness: a common connection in ancient cultures[1, pg 58]

In Judaism, for example, consciousness moved through the *sefirot*, or Kabbalistic centers of spiritual development, the highest being Keter, or Crown. In the Eastern Ayuvedic tradition, these centers are called Chakras, and particular experiences likewise accompany the movement of energy through them. The highest *Chakra* is also called the Crown, or the Thousand-petaled Lotus. In both traditions, the location of this Crown *sefira* or *chakra* is the center and top of the skull, anatomically corresponding to the human pineal gland. Note that the third eye is believed to more closely correspond with the pituitary gland [1, pg 59].

We first read about the physical pineal gland in the writings of Herophilus, a third-century B.C. Greek physician from the time of

Alexander the Great. Its name comes from the Latin pineus, relating to the pine, pinus. This little organ is thus *piniform*, or shaped like a pinecone, no bigger than the nail of your little finger.

The pineal gland is unique in its solitary status within the brain. All other brain sites are paired, meaning that they have left and right counterparts. As the only unpaired organ deep within the brain, the pineal gland remained an anatomical curiosity for nearly two thousand years. No one in the West had any idea what the pineal gland's function was.

Interest in the pineal grew once attracting the attention of Rene Descarte. This famous seventeenth-century French philosopher and mathematician, who said, " I think therefore I am," needed a divine origin for those thoughts. Introspection showed him that it was possible to think only one thought at a time. From where in the brain might these unpaired, solitary thoughts arise? Descartes proposed that the pineal, the only singleton organ of the brain, generated thoughts. In addition, Descartes believed the pineal's location, directly above one of the crucial byways for the cerebrospinal fluid, made this function even more likely.

Hollow cavities deep within the brain termed the ventricles, produce clear, salty, protein-rich cerebrospinal fluid. This fluid protects the brain by cushioning it from sudden jolts and bumps. It also carries nutrients to, and waste products away from deep brain tissue.

In Descarte's view, the ebb and flow of the cerebrospinal fluid through the ventricles seemed logical as the origin of thoughts. If the pineal gland "secreted" thoughts into the cerebrospinal fluid, what better means for the "stream of consciousness" to make its way to the rest of the brain [1, pg 59]

Descartes also had a deeply spiritual side believing that thinking was basically a spiritual phenomenon made possible by our divine nature shared with the Creator. That is, our thoughts are expressions of, and proof for the existence of, our soul. Descartes believed that the pineal gland played an essential role in the expression of the soul.

Descartes thus proposed that the pineal gland somehow was the "seat of the soul." The intermediary between the spiritual and physical. The body and the spirit met there, each affecting the other, and the repercussions extended in both directions [1, pg 60].

Could Descartes be right? What do we know about the biology of the pineal gland and does it relate to the nature of spirit/energy? The pineal gland of evolutionarily older animals, such as lizards and amphibians, is also called the "third" eye. Just like the two seeing eyes, the third eye possesses a lens, cornea, and retina and is light-sensitive. The pineal gland helps regulate body temperature and skin coloration-two basic reptilian survival functions intimately related to environmental light. Melatonin, the primary pineal hormone, is present in primitive pineal glands.

As animals climbed the evolutionary ladder, the pineal moved inward, deeper into the brain, more hidden and removed from outside influences. While the bird pineal no longer sits on top of the skull, it remains sensitive to outside light because of the paper-thin surrounding bones. The mammalian, including human, pineal is buried even deeper in the brain's recesses and is not directly sensitive to light, at least in adults. It is interesting to speculate that as the pineal assumes a more "spiritual" role, it needs the greater protection from the environment afforded by such deep placement in the skull.

The human pineal gland becomes visible in the developing fetus at seven weeks, or forty-nine days, after conception. Of great interest is the fact that coincident with this time is exactly the time at which sexual differentiation is clearly detectable. Before this time the sex of the fetus is indeterminate, or unknown. Thus, the pineal gland and the most important differentiation of humanity, male and female gender, appear at the same time [1, pg 61].

For many years physiologists considered the mammalian pineal gland the equivalent of the "brains appendix." It was a residual, vestigial organ, a throwback to our early reptilian days, with no known role. Functional roles began to appear when American dermatologist Aaron Lerner discovered melatonin in 1958.[1, pg 62]

The full name for Melatonin is N-acetyl-5-methoxy-tryptamine. Note that melatonin is a tryptamine, just like di-methyl-tryptamine or DMT, a very powerful hallucinogen. Noradrenalin and adrenaline are neurotransmitters that control melatonin production in the pineal gland. Only the adrenaline and noradrenalin released by nearby pineal nerve ending have any effect on pineal function.

It is strange that the pineal gland does not originate from brain tissue, and exists outside the blood-brain barrier. The gland should be seemingly responsive to blood-borne chemicals and drugs, but this is not the case as the pineal function is highly protected by the body. Blood-borne neurotransmitters secreted into the blood never get to the pineal gland.

Is it possible that melatonin could be the hormone responsible for the blinding white light mystical experiences aforementioned by Yogis which closely resembled a DMT trip? During abn n FDA facilitated DMT study by Dr. Strassman, a patient was accidently given a high dose of melatonin, the results of which prove that it was not a psychoactive element much to the disappointment of the researchers conducting the study.

The general hypothesis is that the pineal gland produces psychedelic amounts of DMT, the most powerful hallucinogen known on earth, at extraordinary times in our lives [1, pg 68] The DMT produced within the pineal is utilized within the confines of the brain and is prevented from crossing over the blood-brain barrier.

When our individual life force enters our fetal body, the moment in which we become truly human, it passes through the pineal and triggers the first primordial flood of DMT. Later at birth, the pineal releases more DMT. In some of us, pineal DMT mediates the pivotal experiences of deep meditation, psychosis, and near-death experiences. As we die, the life-force leaves the body through the pineal gland, releasing another flood of their psychedelic spirit molecule.

An interesting observation to note is the correlation between the Tibetan Buddhist belief that the soul takes forty nine days after death to collect itself, assess the lessons of its past life, and then chose another [1, pg 61].

This time period matches exactly with two landmark events in the development of the fetus from conception: "Forty-Nine is when the fetus differentiates into male and female gender. It also takes forty-nine days from conception for the first signs of the human pineal to appear and show the presence of DMT." This correlation is significant in that the differentiation into male and female genders occurs biologically at the exact same time that pineal DMT becomes detectable is more than just coincidence. Was this the 7 x 7 (49 days) needed for Enki's being to be infused with the energy that animates humans?

Preserving Anunnaki Life: Starfire Gold

With the biology primer on the pineal gland completed, now consider the rituals that were being performed in the Mesopotamian temples as it relates to evolving human consciousness. Located within the temple of Hathor on Mt Sinai, archaeologist found a large quantity of a white talcum-like powder in a storage chamber beneath a stone in the floor. When analyzed, the white powder turned out to be a by-product of gold processing, which was apparently being formulated into bread and consumed by the temple priests and ritual attendants.

What then is it that can outweigh itself, but can also under weigh itself and become nothing? What then is it that can be gold, but can be turned to a powder? It is the stone of the hidden name, the shem-an-na, the "highward fire-stone" which is none other than the Sumerian firestone of the Master Craftsmen metallurgists [48, pg 129]. The white powdered *starfire* gold was consumed by high-ranking Anunnaki, knowing that it activated the pineal gland, subsequently producing DMT which is somehow correlated to the production of the enzyme telomerase, tempering the damage to telomeres during cell division. A solution to the rapid aging process due to the short solar cycles on Earth had been found. Common reports from Strassman's DMT patients was a feeling of connectedness with a sacred realm, perhaps another frequency dimension that becomes accessible when high levels of DMT exist in the brain. Clearly, for the concoction to work, it had to affect the DNA strand integrity by preventing the telomeres from decaying, as will be discussed in the next chapter. An added hypothetical used for starfire gold could have involved the intentional enhancement of mental or telepathic communications, given the electromagnetic to chemical transduction function Dr. Strassman assigned to the "Sprit Molecule", DMT. In layman's terms, the DMT could convert the electromagnetic waves to thoughts and thoughts to an electromagnetic wave, like a Bluetooth short range modulator/demodulator (MODEM).

Revisiting Exodus, we find a strange account in which Moses himself appears to have the starfire gold recipe, as he converts a golden statue into the elixir of the gods, forcing his followers to drink the DNA-altering solution. Was Moses forcing the spiritually blind to experience the blinding white light of the pineal DMT release, although purportedly short-lived in its transformative effects?

Exodus 32:19 (NIV)

When Moses approached the camp and saw the calf and the dancing, his anger burned and he threw the tablets out of his hands, breaking them to pieces at the foot of the mountain. [20] And he took the calf the people had made and burned it in the fire; then he ground it to powder, scattered it on the water and made the Israelites drink it.

In Chapter 7 the reader will be transported from the realm of energy, matter, and brain science and follow the deeds of King Gilgamesh of the Mesopotamian city of Uruk, as he sought a method to overcome his genetic trappings seeking eternal life given his Anunnaki blood lineage. Apparently he was not influential enough to obtain access to the exclusive Mount Sinai Hathor Temple Club, where they were regularly prolonging their lives smelting the gold the primitive workers mined for them.

7 GILGAMESH, NOAH AND ETERNAL LIFE

The Epic of Gilgamesh is deemed the longest and greatest literary composition written in Akkadian cuneiform script. The narration follows the heroic king of the Sumerian city of Uruk, located in modern day southern Iraq. The heroic king Gilgamesh reached notoriety due to his worldwide recognizable theme: his famed quest for immortality.

Kingship, the sole form of early governorship in Mesopotamia, was ordained by the Anunnaki gods. Kings were considered to be great shepherds, maintaining order, military leadership and security, and performing priestly functions such as creating laws and conducting large scale building projects. Kings also served as the liaison between the gods and the masses. Early kings were likely genetic offspring of the Anunnaki, demigods being a hybrid mix between pure Niburian blood and the diluted genetics concocted for the slave species Adapa.

According to the Sumerian King's List, Lugalbanda called the "Shepherd King", served for 1,200 years as the second king of Uruk. A mythological Sumerian text describes a romantic relationship between Lugalbanda and Ninsun, a full-blooded Anunnaki female goddess. In the *Gilgamesh and Huwawa* tale, the hero consistently uses the phrase: "By the life of my own mother Ninsun and of my father, holy Lugalbanda!" Thus, it is clear that king Gilgamesh had royal Anunnaki blood, three quarters pure to be more exact. Lugalbanda may have preceded Gilgamesh as king and father, but he was merely a human. Ninsun, being a full-blooded Anunnaki female, would contribute mitochondrial DNA in addition to her reproductive material, making her offspring ¾ Anunnaki. This is the reason behind the Niburian inheritance rules predicating that the rightful heir is produced from the father and his half sister, perpetuating dominating effects of mitochondrial DNA in the progeny. Table 5 below depicts the First Dynasty Kings of Uruk. The lineage data shows that although Gilgamesh was King circa 2600 BCE and ruled for 126 years, he did not follow in direct succession after his father Lugalbanda, but rather succeeded Dumuzi, a son of Enki.

Ruler	Epithet	Length of Reign	Approx. dates	Comments
Mesh-ki-ang-gasher of E-ana	*"the son of Utu"*	324 years	ca. 27th	
"Mesh-ki-ang-gasher entered the sea and disappeared."				
Enmerkar	*"the son of Mesh-ki-ang-gasher, the king of Unug, who built Unug (Uruk)"*	420 years		
Lugalbanda	*"the shepherd"*	1200 years		
Dumuzid (Dumuzi)	*"the fisherman whose city was Kuara."* (*"He captured En-me-barage-si single-handed."*)*	100 years	ca. 2600 BCE	
Gilgamesh	*"whose father was a phantom (?), the lord of Kulaba"*	126 years	ca. 2600 BCE	contemporary with Aga of Kish, according to the Epic of

				Gilgamesh[1]
Ur-Nungal	*"the son of Gilgamesh"*	30 years		
Udul-kalama	*"the son of Ur-Nungal"*	15 years		
La-ba'shum		9 years		
En-nun-tarah-ana		8 years		
Mesh-he	*"the smith"*	36 years		
Melem-ana		6 years		
Lugal-kitun		36 years		
"Then Unug was defeated and the kingship was taken to Urim (Ur)."				

Table 5: Kings of Uruk

Wide geographic discovery of the tablets relating to the Gilgamesh epic occurred throughout the Middle East, with concentrations found in the late second millennium BCE. Samples included tablets found in Megiddo written in Akkadian. Others were found in Emar on the mid-Euphrates. Versions were found in Akkadian, Hittite, and Hurrian languages discussed at Hatusas Hittite capital in Northern Anatolia. Versions found in Nineveh in the seventh century were dated to a time during the Kasite Kingship of Senacherib.

No one knows why the famous epic was written, but its introduction to the contemporary gods of Mesopotamia coincides with the names used in the Atrahasis, including the major members of the Anunnaki Council: namely Enlil, Enki, and Anu. Gilgamesh's heroic and emotion laden quest for eternal life, like his Anunnaki ancestors possessed, appealed to audiences for centuries throughout the entire region. Gilgamesh knew as king that the humans created by Enki had a limited lifespan to only 120 years. The sensitive king anguished over the loss of life, and dreadfully feared his own death because of his genetic lack, although demigods like the lucky king lived far longer than 120 years, as evidenced by the long lives annotated in Genesis 4 and his many deeds in ancient Mesopotamia.

The Anunnaki were partaking of life prolonging star fire gold to mitigate the effects of the rapid solar cycles experienced on earth in order to prevent their telomeres from deteriorating [48, pg 253]. Thus the Anunnaki appeared immortal to humans or to have everlasting life. The records do not indicate that king Gilgamesh was afforded the same life prolonging luxury. Gilgamesh knew that because of his diluted Anunnaki blood that he would not be afforded the same eternal lifespan of his mother Ninsun.

Press Release 2009-10-05

The Nobel Assembly at Karolinska Institutet has today decided to award

The Nobel Prize in Physiology or Medicine 2009

jointly to

Elizabeth H. Blackburn, Carol W. Greider and Jack W. Szostak

for the discovery of

**"how chromosomes are protected
by telomeres and the enzyme telomerase"**

Brief mention was published about the Nobel Prize winning scientists Blackburn, Greider and Szostak; whose research on human chromosomes, and the effects that telomere deterioration, or lack thereof, has on human aging, were awarded the Nobel Prize in the year 2009.

The Nobel Prize in Physiology or Medicine was awarded to the scientists having solved a major problem in biology: how the chromosomes can be copied during cell divisions without suffering degradation. The Nobel Laureates found the that enzyme telomerase helps protect telomeres from aging.

The long, thread-like DNA molecules that carry our genes are packed into chromosomes, the telomeres being the caps on their ends. Elizabeth Blackburn and Jack Szostak discovered that a unique DNA sequence in the telomeres protects the chromosomes from degradation. Carol Greider and Elizabeth Blackburn identified telomerase, the enzyme that makes telomere DNA. These discoveries explained how the ends of the chromosomes are protected by the telomeres and that they are built by telomerase.

If the telomeres are shortened, cells age. Conversely, if telomerase activity is high, telomere length is maintained, and cellular damage is delayed. This is the case in cancer cells, which can be considered to have eternal life. Certain inherited diseases, in contrast, are characterized by a defective telomerase, resulting in damaged cells. The award of the Nobel Prize recognizes the discovery of a fundamental mechanism in the cell, a discovery that has stimulated the development of new therapeutic strategies. Seems like ancient knowledge about anti-aging is just now being re-discovered. The Anunnaki mention aging as a problem for them on Earth.

They found solutions, the ultimate being starfire gold, reserved for the elite. It would be interesting to do a comparative study using modern medical techniques to determine the precursors for telomerase as discussed in the 2009 Nobel Prize research.

Being king has its perks. One of which, tantalizing as it must have been for Gilgamesh, was having access to otherwise forbidden knowledge kept by the alien astronauts in his own backyard of Uruk. Inanna and Anu both had temples in Uruk. The Anunnaki guarded the ME's, which were reported to be 94 in total containing, information for the ancient astronauts to roll out the full aspects of civilizations on a remote planet. The knowledge stored on these ME tablets, most likely contained technical details about genetics and their link to what seemed to be eternal *life spans* lived by the gods.

The extent to which Gilgamesh knew about the role genetics played in long life, as witnessed by the longevity of the Anunnaki enshrined as gods and deified in Mesopotamia, propelled him in the quest to obtain it for himself. Following the last great deluge to hit Mesopotamia, *of which there was more than one*, Ziusudra (AKA Atrahasis/Noah) and his family landed on Mount Ararat aboard his famed ark, as instructed by his father Enki. Enlil, while soaring aloft along with several other Anunnaki key figures surveying flood damage, spotted Ziusudra and his ark and was infuriated that one or more of the humans had survived the catastrophe. Later that evening, while conducting an offering at an impromptu altar he built onsite, Ziusudra had an encounter with Enlil and Enki where the truth of his bloodline is revealed. Enki admits that he is Ziusudra's father, and that is why he saved him from the destructive deluge.

It is during that encounter with Enlil, that Ziusudra, only 50% pure in his Anunnaki lineage, was granted access to eternal life. The details of what transpired on the mountain are not completely clear, but using the precedence provided in the Anunnaki writings, most likely involved a Council decision to provide access to a specific "plant of life" for the transformed and newly renamed Anunnaki club member, Ut-napishtim.

When Dumuzi and Ningishzida escorted the Adapa to meet Anu in heaven/Nibiru [14, pg 178], as part of the ritual encounter offered by a Niburian host, the bread of life and the elixir of life are offered by Anu but refused by the mortal slave Adapa in accordance with Enki's wishes. These concoctions were more than likely devised to overcome the damage done to Anunnaki DNA eternally perpetuating the biological renewal process. This telomere renewal process appears to have been replicated or re-engineered on Earth given the rapid aging discussed by the Anunnaki working the mines for long durations in Africa. Gilgamesh sought a plant of life that produced the same life-prolonging effects.

Failing in his Baalbek with the god in Lebanon [70], king Gilgamesh contrived a plan to find Enki's son Ziusudra, who was renamed Ut-napishtim following his changed longevity status and being allowed into the "god's private club." If Gilgamesh could find the king of Shurrupak, Ziusudra to the Sumerians, Noah to the readers of the Canonical Bible, then he could find out the secret given to him by Enlil atop Mount Ararat and achieve eternal life for himself too. After all, Ziusudra only had 50% pure blood and Gilgamesh had 75% pure Anunnaki lineage. Thus, it only seemed right to Ninsun's boy Gilgamesh that he should be entitled to the same treatment. This is the catalyst for Gilgamesh's epic tale and the background situation in Uruk approximately 2600 BCE.

At the expense of doing injustice to the entire Epic, it will not be offered as a summarized tale beyond the analysis provided herein. Several printed and online translations of the Epic of Gilgamesh are readily available to the researcher. I have a friend whose fifth-grade child was attending a private school where I reside in San Diego, California. One of the reading assignments given to the youth enrolled over the summer session was the Epic of Gilgamesh, much to my surprise and amazement. Most Americans would struggle to differentiate Turkey from Iraq geographically, none the less partake of classic Middle Eastern Literature like the one originating in the astounding culture of Sumeria, modern civilization's genesis [41,43]. *It is no wonder parents want their children educated in private schools* where the NEA approved story of modern history is not passed through the editorial scruples of the government's story tellers prior to landing on the public furnished desks at our kid's neighborhood school.

With that said, king Gilgamesh finds the great flood exiled Ut-napishtim in his quest and gets him to relate the details about the plant of life he seeks, which is harvested in the shallow waters of the ocean.

Epic of Gilgamesh, Tablet XI [37, pg 109]

Gilgamesh spoke to him, to Ut-napishtim, the far-distant.

"I look at you, Ut-napishtim

And your limbs are no different-you are just like me.

Indeed, you are not at all different-you are just like me.

I feel the urge to prove myself against you, to pick a fight."

Ut-napishtim spoke to him, to Gilgamesh,

"Let me reveal to you a closely guarded matter, Gilgamesh,

And let me tell you the secret of the gods."

From this point, the Biblical Noah tells Gilgamesh the full detailed accounting of what happened before, during, and after the great flood. Compare this accounting to that told in Genesis 7-9. Hmm, quite a different accounting of a story that was so important in the search for mankind's true origins.

Epic of Gilgamesh, Tablet XI [37, pg 109]

Shurrupak is a city that you yourself know,

Situated on the bank of the Euphrates.

That city was already old when the gods within it

Decided that the great gods should make a flood.

There was Anu their father,

Warrior Ellil their counselor,

Ninurta was their chamberlain,

Ennugi their canal-controller,

Far-sighted Ea swore the oath of secrecy with them.

So he repeated their speech to a reed hut,

"Reed hut, reed hut, brick wall, brick wall,

Listen, reed hut and pay attention, brick wall:

Man of Shurrupak, son of Ubara-Tutu,

Dismantle your house, build a boat.

Leave possessions, search out living things.

Reject cattle and save lives!

Put aboard the seed of all living things, into the boat."

(gap)

I realized and spoke to my master Ea,

"I have paid attention to the words that you spoke in this way,

My master, and I shall act upon them.

But how can I explain myself to the city, the men and the elders?"

Ea (Enki) made his voice heard and spoke,

He said to me, his servant,

"You shall speak to them thus:

I think that Ellil has rejected me,

And so I cannot stay in your city,

And I cannot set foot on Ellis's land again.

I must go down to the Apsu and stay with my master Ea."

The important point of this Tablet XI snippet, is to point out that Ut-napishtim attributes his fate to his father Enki who warned him of the upcoming flood and Enlil, for blessing him with eternal life.

Ut-napishtim and the king of Uruk go on a hunt for the heralded plant of life, find it, and Gilgamesh heads home via the sea with his prize plant. Given the symbols alluded to in the Epic, those officially ascribed to Enki, lord of the waters, the plant is taken away from Gilgamesh, indicating Enki's original genetic design constraining mankind to a finite life span, namely 120 years. Even though Gilgamesh was more than likely to live well beyond the mere mortal lifespan cap, his destiny was not to be immortal like Noah and the gods. A similar hero of old, Alexander the Great of Macedonia, suffered the exact same dilemma and consequences as Gilgamesh. Both demigods perished here on earth, heroes of old, men of renown as described in the Hebrew edited version of the Bible, New International Version.

Genesis 6:4 (NIV)

The Nephilim were on the earth in those days—and also afterward—when the sons of God went to the daughters of men and had had children by them. They were the heroes of old, the men of renown.

Gilgamesh's Mother, Ninsun, would be a terrific candidate to study for the genealogy of the Anunnaki since she had a pure blood line. The mother of a hero of old, a king of great renown. Obviously, having knowledge about Gilgamesh's grave site makes one wonder where his DNA analysis report is filed and who has access to it? See the press release published in 2003. A press release from the BBC is provided shortly.

As for other deeds the hero Gilgamesh accomplished, also known as Nimrod in the Bible, again from Genesis we have the following details:

Genesis 10:8-12 (NIV)

Cush was the father of Nimrod, who grew to be a mighty warrior on the earth, He was a mighty hunter before the Lord; that is why it is said "like Nimrod, a mighty hunter before the Lord." The first centers *of his kingdom were Babylon, Erech (Uruk), Akkad and Calneh, in Shinar (Sumer). From that land he went to Assyria, where he built Nineveh, Rehoboth Ir, Calah and Resen, which is between Nineveh and Calah; that is the great city.*

Zecharia Sitchin dreamt of having an ancient astronaut's body from Nibiru genetically analyzed, validating his hypothesis on the Sumerian gods, hopefully in his lifetime. I was listening to a program via YouTube last week and heard an old pre-recorded program shown in which Zecharia Sitchin was being interviewed, and the aged and soft-spoken scholar mentioned on the Coast to Coast AM Radio program with George Noory, his expressed desire to see his theories validated with science correlating mankind's missing link origins with the archetypal entwined serpent strands of Anunnaki DNA. Perhaps the "junk" human DNA [86], of which approximately 95% of it has been deemed by science for lack of understanding, was part of the original Anunnaki DNA that had been inactivated in the primitive workers. Comparing the original Anunnaki DNA with human DNA would most likely dispel any further reservations about the Anunnaki genesis for humanity's creation. In my humble opinion, given the fact that grave sites have been unearthed and physical anthropology has been focused on the Sumer region since the turn of the century, this DNA analysis has long been accomplished. The results of such a study would certainly be hidden knowledge from the masses.

Saddam Hussein hired a team of German archeologists to find Gilgamesh's grave in the city of Uruk. The city was mapped using a magnetometer [68] as reported in a press release from the BBC April 2003 [74].

Gilgamesh tomb believed found

Story from BBC NEWS:
http://news.bbc.co.uk/go/pr/fr/-
/2/hi/science/nature/2982891.stm

Published: 2003/04/29 07:57:11 GMT

Archaeologists in Iraq believe they may have found the lost tomb of King Gilgamesh – the subject of the oldest "book" in history.

The Epic Of Gilgamesh – written by a Middle Eastern scholar 2,500 years before the birth of Christ – commemorated the life of the ruler of the city of Uruk, from which Iraq gets its name.

Now, a German-led expedition has discovered what is thought to be the entire city of Uruk – including, where the Euphrates once flowed, the last resting place of its famous King.

"I don't want to say definitely it was the grave of King Gilgamesh, but it looks very similar to that described in the epic," Jorg Fassbinder, of the Bavarian department of Historical Monuments in Munich, told the BBC World Service's Science in Action programme.

Magnetic

In the book – actually a set of inscribed clay tablets – Gilgamesh was described as having been buried under the Euphrates, in a tomb apparently constructed when the waters of the ancient river parted following his death.

"We found just outside the city an area in the middle of the former Euphrates river, the remains of such a building which could be interpreted as a burial," Mr Fassbinder said.

He said the amazing discovery of the ancient city under the Iraqi desert had been made possible by modern technology.

"By differences in magnetization in the soil, you can look into the ground," Mr Fassbinder added.

"The difference between mud bricks and sediments in the Euphrates river gives a very detailed structure."

This creates a magnetogram, which is then digitally mapped, effectively giving a town plan of Uruk.

'Venice in the desert'

"The most surprising thing was that we found structures already described by Gilgamesh," Mr Fassbinder stated.

"We covered more than 100 hectares. We have found garden structures and field structures as described in the epic, and we found Babylonian houses."

But he said the most astonishing find was an incredibly sophisticated system of canals.

"Very clearly, we can see in the canals some structures showing that flooding destroyed some houses, which means it was a highly developed system.

"[It was] like Venice in the desert."

The temple complexes in Uruk were specified as the Eanna District and the Anu District, both of which were dedicated to the Anunnaki gods and Council members Inanna and Anu, respectively. The Anu District dates back to the times of Eridu, considered to be one of the oldest and most important cities of Sumer. Temples served both an important religious function and state functions. Gilgamesh's direct knowledge and interaction with the likes of Inanna and Anu make the story even more compelling. These are not conjured up gods, but living beings that regularly visit Uruk and take residence in their impressive temples therein.

Saddam Hussein's interest in rebuilding Babylon, Marduk's *gateway of the gods*, was supposedly driven by his belief that he was a reincarnation of Nebuchadnezzar [75]. Also, he hired a team of Germans to run a magnetometer over the ancient site of Uruk, during the first Gulf war in 1991. In order to gain access to the site, a massive bypass canal was built to divert the water where the famous reeds grew, away from the Uruk area. This dried up the region allowing easy archeological access. This domestic archeological digging activity seemed somewhat crazy to be focused on while being overthrown by the world's most powerful military, the United States of America?

An independent archaeologist that discussed a direct link between the ancient ET presence in Sumer and the US focus on the regime of Saddam Hussein, is William Henry. Henry's main thesis was that there existed in Sumerian times a 'Stargate', used by the Anunnaki/Nephilim to travel back and forth between Nibiru and the Earth [53]. Henry focuses on the following scene described by Sitchin's interpretation of a cuneiform tablet of an Uruk ritual text:

"Depictions have been found that show divine beings flanking a temple entrance and holding up poles to which ring-like objects are attached. The celestial nature of the scene is indicated by the inclusion of the symbols of the Sun and the Moon.... depicting Enlil and Enki flanking a gateway through which Anu is making a grand entrance."

Rather than a simple temple scene involving the chief Anunnaki of the Sumerians, Anu and his two sons, Enlil and Enki, Henry proposes that the above scene represents a transportation device used by Anu and others from the elite Anunnaki. If so, then such a device is most likely located in the Sumerian city of Uruk [75], which was the founding city of the Sumerian civilization, and the home of Gilgamesh, the famed king of the Epic of Gilgamesh. Could this explain Saddam Hussein's interest in mapping out the city of Uruk? Saddam's secret agenda involving Sumerian artifacts died with him, and we may never know the truth, lest Anu or some other high ranking Anunnaki re-activates the portal in Uruk or Jerusalem with news media crews present, and introduces themselves to the world via some talk show program on television.

8 EVOLUTION OF HUMAN CONSCIOUSNESS SUPPRESSED

"Realize deeply that the present moment is all you have. Make the NOW the primary focus of your life." Eckhart Tolle from the "Power of Now" [23].

It should be clear to peoples of the world that modern governments do not want the evolution of human consciousness to occur; and especially not the extension of one's life: This negative disposition between the governors and the serfs originated with Enlil. Evidence abounds in the world's cultures that perpetuate chemical enslavement abiding by government established mores; the latest of which involves the likes of Monsanto and its team of lawyers accosting the world's food supply with genetically modified foods/organisms (GMO) shown to cause significant harm in a recent finding involving pigs, whose digestive tract is quite similar to humans. According to the study, researchers found a statistically significant increase in severe stomach inflammation; about 2.5 times higher in the pigs that were fed the engineered grains compared to the non-engineered grains. Additionally, the weight of a pig's uterus was 25 percent larger for GM-fed pigs, an issue which can lead to problems with a pig's reproductive or hormonal system, said Michael Hansen, Consumer's Union Senior Staff scientist [110]. The next section details some of the modern chemicals humans have a close relationship to, helping governments around the world keep human consciousness suppressed to its lowest Root Chakra level. For a good laugh, consider watching the movie "Idiocracy", a 2006 satirical science fiction comedy that makes fun of the human mob, crawling beneath the rotting seats at the lowest level of human existence, worse than Plato's allegorical projection on the "he said, she said" cave wall. You will laugh, and nod your head in conciliatory cultural disgust.

Enslavement Techniques

Methods used by the Ancient gods and modern governments to enslave mankind are many. Slavery imposed upon the primitive workers was done readily achieved using in-vitro fertilization: mixing Enki's DNA with the female zygote of a primitive bi-pedal hominid, found roaming the plains of South Africa approximately 200,000 years ago. Aside from the physical suppression of consciousness by anatomically modern human genetic craftsmen, other means for controlling the growing world's population would be necessary as the tenets of civilization were slowly introduced to mankind by the Anunnaki. The instructions for seeding new civilizations on alien planets existed, according to the Sumerian texts, in the form of tablets or information disks simply referred to in the texts as ME's, of which there were a total of 94. These "*recipe disks*" containing the details for implementing components of civilization were kept by Enki personally, either in his cult center temple in Eridu or in Southeastern Africa where his mining headquarters was established.

Economic Enslavement

Suppose there were a population of primitive workers that the Anunnaki had decided to introduce to the usury system, initially needed for ancient trade, marriage records, and general accounting techniques. Further suppose that the genetic capabilities available to the primitive workers was originally quite pure and was tailored genetically to produce a specific functional capability such as procedural knowledge specific to the acts of mining and temple and city-building. *A major concern would be to get the primitive workers to do somewhat sophisticated work while at the same time suppressing the behavior or propensity to revolt after enduring extreme hard labor.*

It should be obvious to the casual observer that economic disparity is a function of the capabilities of the individual relative to a usury system that highly values and rewards certain capabilities while at the same time providing only a meager existence to those that do not have the desired skills or goods. An example in our modern society is offered. Consider the economic earning difference that exists between Nobel prize winning scientists and someone that has a learning disability that precludes them from attending a higher learning institute. The former may earn many times more than their struggling counterpart. Many such instances can be imagined across a spectrum of vignettes. The issue at hand is the unfairness of the economic system that bases one's earning potential to a large part on genetics, not to overlook the environment as a contributing factor as well. The usury system could only be considered fair if all men were truly created equal, which is not the case at all. If one doubts this statement, compare the wages earned for highly technical workers like engineers, scientists, and computer programmer with the earning potential of laborers in the fast food industry. News media reports that these workers are joining unions and striking en mass due to the fact that they cannot earn a living wage in the fast food business. We may be born with the notion of equal access to opportunity in society, but not equal intellect or innate abilities to access it. Would the likes of Einstein's intellect be equivalent to that of a common factory worker? Of course not, and the ability to earn an equal income in a usury system that assumes that by merely having "equal access to opportunities" makes the system fair is absurd. In large part, due to the innate differences in ability, the majority of those in society are essentially *relegated to economic slavery, disguised as a free system.* A working class individual that must rely on the usury system to pay for housing, food, clothing, and medical care, often lives from paycheck to paycheck unable to save money and work their way out of the economic trap. If the commoner is focused on making a living to simply survive in the system, the likelihood of working toward an elevated consciousness, considered dangerous by the ruling class, is practically null and void. Traditionally, the source of dissidents and uprisings comes from the highly educated and not from the class of economic slaves. Although hard labor and difficult toil has been the basis of physical mutiny against the immediate enslavers, the ability to organize and incite a large group to action has historically eluded the pauper enslaved class.

Throughout history ruling class tactics have used a multitude of control methods to prevent "mob uprisings", a noteworthy advisor to kings was Machiavelli, who authored "The Prince", a series of advice-lessons provided to French rulers as regarding interactions of a ruler with his followers. Later civilizations adopted alternative methods to keep the mob at bay. One such method used in Rome was to pacify the mob by entertaining them: a continuous calendar of events scheduled in the now infamous Coliseum to provide a passive outlet for pent up frustrations that otherwise would surface and be directed towards the ruling class. Free entertainment surely is alluring, but other methods exist at various levels in a society designed to ensure compliance with ruling class mores or laws. Terrence McKenna, in his book *"Food of the Gods"* [4] discusses chemicals that were supported in early trade routes throughout the world *that populations found irresistible and rulers appreciated as the chemical substances had suppressive or dulling effects on human consciousness.* Alternative consciousness suppression techniques included modern approaches to the energy and matter interactions discussed in Chapter 6; specifically the effects ELF can have on controlling the human mind.

Conscious Suppressing Chemicals

The ways in which humans use plants, foods, and drugs causes the values of individuals and, ultimately, whole societies to shift. Eating some foods makes folks happy while eating others makes one sleepy, and still others cause alertness. Society encourages consumption of substances by the population that produce acceptable behavior.

"Like fish in water, people in a culture swim in the virtually invisible medium of culturally sanctioned yet artificial states of mind." [4] This hidden yet powerful chemical dependency was promoted if the effects of the substance made subjects happy and more controllable, otherwise the substances were made illegal by the ruling class. Examples include hallucinogens such as mushrooms that contain psilocybin, potentially causing primitive workers to become aware of their own nakedness upon consumption?

As sugar and other spices found their way into the trade routes that served Europeans, having endured a dismal and boring existence sans lavish colors and variety, the Middle Ages were brought to an end. Christian medieval Europe broke up as a result of the consciousness expanding chemicals that entered the market: coffee, opium dyes, silks, and rare gems were put on display in the public forum. The new trade goods were exotic and delightful. Sugar, chocolate, tea and coffee, and distilled alcohol survive to this day as staples of the modern world. Our global trading market was created to cater to society's need for variety and stimulation, *especially when it comes to food*. One particular drug that found ready acceptance in medieval Europe was cane sugar [4].

The Romans favored sugar but knew that the bamboo-like grass from which sugar was refined grew only in tropical regions, making it a rare and imported commodity. Sugar beets were encouraged by Napoleon I as an alternative to the hard to get cane sugar.

Sugar abuse is the world's least discussed and most widespread addiction [4]. Sugar, as with all stimulants, causes a brief euphoric rush that is shortly followed by depression, guilt, and usually an upset stomach if the individual quantity threshold is exceeded. Sugar abuse is often correlated with serious alcohol consumption. Sugar and slavery are also closely related. Sugar cane grew in tropical regions and had to be imported, which led to brutal kidnappings, forced transporting, and mass murder of huge populations enslaved by merchants to support the addictive and growing demand for cane sugar.

The use of tobacco in Europe in the sixteenth century has been perpetuated on a global scale, although smoking tobacco in the form of cigarettes in the United States, especially in coastal health conscious areas, has been the target of government sponsored negative advertising campaigns and has been banned in many public places. Developing nations and those on various trajectories along the industrialization curve are the heaviest tobacco users.

With the arrival of Europeans, tobacco became one of the primary products fueling the colonization of the future American South, long before the creation of the United States. The initial colonial expansion, fueled by the desire to increase tobacco production, was one cause of the first colonial conflicts with Native Americans and became a driving factor for the use of African slave labor. Nothing complements a good smoke like a hard shot to wash down the tar and nicotine. Next we will look at alcohol's effects on human consciousness.

Alcohol may be responsible for suppressing inhibitions leading to more dynamic human interactions at the local pub, but it is not likely to be associated with elevation of consciousness any time soon, nor was it deemed so in the distant past [95-107]. The effects of alcohol vary from person to person and with different amounts. The number of drinks that constitute being "drunk" for one person may have little effect on another. Also varying are the changes in behavior that one undergoes when under the influence of alcohol. A person may behave in a way that is quite unlike their usual personality. For instance, someone who is normally calm and collected may become easily enraged and upset or vice versa. Sometimes the effects of alcohol consumption are more subtle. Someone may simply become quiet and withdrawn. Often these changes are not necessarily dangerous or problematic, but there are times when they certainly can be. Some of the more serious changes in behavior may include violent tendencies, inability to make good or safe decisions, or lack of use of protection when engaging in sexual encounters.

People often drink to relax, to gain confidence, or to be at ease in social situations [96]. Studies show that alcohol intoxication can make us aggressive [106,107]; it can relieve stressful anxiety and tension yet also increase them both; it can inflate our egos yet lead to "crying-in-one's beer" depression [97].

Every time alcohol is consumed, in every person, perception and thought are generally impaired [99]. Research has shown that alcohol intoxication impairs nearly every aspect of information processing: the ability to abstract and conceptualize, the ability to encode large numbers of situational cues, the ability to use several cues at the same time, the use of the active and systematic encoding strategies, and the cognitive elaboration needed to encode meaning from incoming information. Alcohol dulls the senses preventing one from using sensory cues to initiate a proper response, which could be fatal under certain circumstances like drinking and driving.

The consumption of alcohol may radically alter both one's ability and one's motivation to process information regarding sexual risk. Alcohol intoxication can decrease one's ability to consider the consequences of their actions and it can also lower inhibitions about sexual behaviors. Often times, alcohol plays the role of scapegoat, as irresponsible actions can be blamed on the amount of alcohol that was consumed.

In general, studies have shown that people who regularly consume alcohol or use drugs are more likely to engage in high-risk sexual behavior. Leigh and Morrison (1991) report that 50% of both male and female adolescents had been drinking at the time of their first sexual experience.

Alcohol intoxication at the time of first sexual intercourse is associated with a decrease in condom use [100]. Under the influence of alcohol, people often make the poor decision to engage in sexual activity with someone they may not know and then make the even worse decision not to use protection [101]. The basic effects of alcohol on the human awareness and behavior are clearly not conducive to an elevated consciousness.

Other substances that made their way into civilizations via trade merchants recognizing a societal need or want and filling it. The point that needs to be made is that the chemicals and substances that were allowed to stay in circulation in societies were either approved or denied by the ruling powers, with *consciousness suppression being a foremost goal*. Of particular concern to all ruling classes is the potential for an uprising or revolt against the government. With this potential threat foremost in mind, it was and still is imperative to pay particular heed to the chemicals that the population is consuming.

The ideal substance that a ruler would gladly support is one that relegates the population loyal to the ruler, suppresses the urge to revolt even under the most difficult circumstances, and at the same time keeps the subject at a functional level for the tasks assigned. The quintessential consumable substance is one that prevents the ruler's subject from "waking up" to the degree to which the ruling class is exploiting the commoner for his own gain, as is common practice in master-slave relationships both individually and within larger societal settings. Thus, it is to be expected to see substances in circulation that suppress human consciousness, while at the same time outlawing those that elevate consciousness. Sugar, tobacco, alcohol, and caffeine are all prevalent in modern societies, while substances that were traditionally used by Native Americans to elevate-shift consciousness such as mushrooms, peyote, and cannabis are outlawed in the United States today. Some states provide means for societal members to access these substances for medicinal or spiritual purposes, but these are only exceptions to the existing laws that generally outlaw their use by people.

Human Structure and Consciousness

The structural state for most human beings, beginning at birth and continuing throughout the remainder of their life, is definitely a fallen state. Consider the evolutionary path anatomically modern humans have traversed. Our first bipedal ancestors appear to have transitioned from walking on all fours to a more or less upright stance approximately 3.5 million years ago given the state of our current knowledge in the field of physical anthropology. What is meant by the assertion that humans are structurally in a fallen state? And what could that "fallen state" possibly have to do with consciousness?

Structural Integration models the human body as a series of blocks that must stack upon each other in the gravitational field in such a way that there is balance [117]. A working model of the human structure can be delineated accordingly. Beginning from the ground, blocks representing various parts of the body can be represented as stacked one on top of the other. The feet, legs, pelvis, torso, neck, and head are sufficient stackable block representations to demonstrate the point asserted above that most humans are unstructured. Structural integrators use various lines and planes to assess the degree to which the human body is structured in the gravitational field.

A very useful line used to assess human structure, as viewed from the side while standing, begins at the opening of the ear, passes through the shoulder and then the hip socket, progresses to the knee and finally ends at the ankle bone on the outside of the leg. See Figure 13, leftmost image. For those more inclined to use Latin, the line extends from the Auditory Miatus to the Glenoid Fossa to the Acetabulum to the Fibular head and finally to the Lateral Malleolis. Note that the line only passes through bone at the top of the head, passing through the center of gravity behind the pubic bone in the pelvis. In order for a human to be able to stand in a relaxed state and have the aforementioned blocks aligned is a very rare occurrence indeed. For that matter, over time, the human structure exposed to the gravitational field tends to deviate further and further from the imaginary line as described. See Figure 13 for some common human structural patterns.

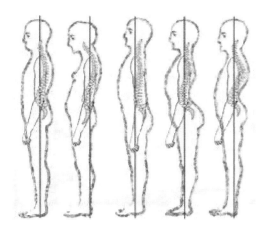

Figure 13: Human Structural Patterns

It's as if the human structure has not evolved far enough to find the gravitational balance point while standing. There are key areas of the body that tend to deter the ability to find this balanced state. Some of the key locations that affect the body's ability to find the vertical line are the Calcaneous or heel, the crest of the Ilium, and the Occipital muscles located at the back of the cranium. Consider that at birth there are tissue disorganizations at these locations that prevent the bony structure from relaxing and aligning with gravity. This is precisely the case in most humans at this present state of evolution having 1st hand knowledge with clients. From birth, if the crest of the Ilium has fascial attachments that prevent the pelvis from being horizontal, rest assured that as the baby transitions from crawling to standing that the pelvis will most likely have an anterior tilt, which is the most common condition found among humans by structural integrators. If the pelvic block is tilted, even slightly anterior, then the blocks above the pelvis will have to adjust to keep the blocks stacked in the very strong gravitational field. To counter balance a tilted pelvis, the torso and head blocks in our model will adjust to compensate for the pelvis. Over time, one can expect to see an anterior head carry when referencing the Auditory Miatus (ear opening) to the Glenoid Fossa otherwise known as the shoulder joint. In time, the anterior head position will stress the upper back muscles, in particular the Trapezoids and the Rhomboids, leading eventually to a kyphotic hump at cervical vertebrae seven (C7). There are other unstructured patterns that emerge based on the degree of fascial disorganization at the occipitals and Calcaneous.

The point of this foray into human structure is to bring awareness to the fallen state of human matter relative to the gravitational field. So what is the effect of an unstructured body? This is where practitioners of yoga and other disciplines like Tai Chi have an experiential understanding of the importance of synchronizing and balancing the human structure in the gravitational field. *Through the process of re-ordering the human structure, practitioners realize empirically that the structural body state has a direct correlation with energy and consciousness.* Strength, balance, flexibility, and consciousness are very much a function of proper structure. It is thus asserted that most ordinary people that have not taken definitive steps to synchronize their bodies within the powerful gravitational field are most likely having or will have pain in their bodies due to an ever-increasing unstructured state. Failing to synchronize the body with the strong gravity field creates a physical limitation preventing the integration of energy and matter-handicapping the individual's ability to reach higher consciousness states.

This slow-motion hardening of the fascia state occurs naturally, without imposing the compounding effects of accidents and poor posture. By the time a child has reached the age of seven or so, sans structural intervention, he or she will not be able to abide by their parental prodding to sit up straight. Additionally, without proper parental or structural guidance to plant the Sacral Ischial Tuberocities (SITS bones) located at the inferior points of the pelvis on the sitting surface, the child will not find balance sitting and will further exacerbate the structural disorder emanating from the all-important pelvis.

In other words, unless a child is taught how to sit correctly early on, assuming a perfect structure to work with, he or she will cause further disorder among the stacked blocks by excessive and improper sitting habits. Gravity always wins this structural battle with the human body. Seeing this fallen condition from a structural standpoint, among the human population at large, is debilitating at best and tragic in its effects on human consciousness which cannot progress beyond what the body's structure allows. An analogy of the unstructured human body to a broken radio antenna is conjured up in the author's mind. If economic disparity, addictive chemical staple substances, and unstructured bodies are not enough to suppress human consciousness on a grand scale, then active interference in the brain using targeted frequencies by repressive governments may be just what doctor Frankenstein ordered.

Frequency Control

Biological components of the human brain that are susceptible to the electromagnetic spectrum as previously detailed. As discussed in Chapter 5, the reticular activating system (RAS), an organ within the human brain, is responsible for focusing attention. It is well know that the human brain registers frequencies in the range 0-20 Hz as recorded and displayed on medical devices such as the electroencephalogram (EEG).

The question raised for the reader's consideration is this: what happens to the human brain, and in particular the RAS, when exposed to external frequencies that fall within this EEG range? Additionally, can information be modulated onto the external frequency that is demodulated biologically by humans, thereby placing "subconscious thoughts" within the human mind? An analogous situation occurs in time of war dealing with enemy use of the electromagnetic spectrum. Battlefield tactics involving radio and navigation equipment are often subversive in nature. For instance, a pilot patrolling a border region may rely on the aircraft instruments to determine the location of friendly beacons located within the borders of the patrolled country. The enemy may desire to draw the pilot across the border so that an engagement may take place without violating international laws by shooting across the border. One way to do this is to use a false frequency originating from across the border to trick the pilot into believing that the navigation device or beacon is friendly. This can be accomplished by methods of *meaconing*, intrusion, jamming, or interference.

Meaconing is the use of a false beacon to fool the enemy into a false sense of security relying on the aircraft instruments, picking up a signal at the same frequency as the actual friendly beacon, but at a high enough intensity to jam the original signal that may be many miles away. Intrusion is a subversive frequency tactic to place false information on a friendly net. Jamming is a method whereby the foe's communication channel is overridden by a higher intensity frequency originating from the enemy. An abbreviated version of totally jamming a channel is to do it intermittently, interfering at critical communication junctures to disrupt the flow of information, normally during a battle sequence. These methods work very well against radio and navigation equipment, so what are the effects of using these subversive electromagnetic tactics against the human brain? Believe it or not, the government of the United States has such a program and has built antennae networks in America to affect human consciousness on a massive scale.

HAARP

The U.S. Senate funded an ongoing project called the High frequency Active Auroral Research Program otherwise known as HAARP. The stated goal for the HAARP program is to further advance knowledge of the physical and electrical properties of the Earth's ionosphere, which according to information from the official website (http://www.haarp.alaska.edu/) can affect military and civilian communication and navigation systems. The HAARP program operates a world-class ionospheric research facility located in Gakona, Alaska. HAARP is jointly managed by the U.S. Air Force Phillips Laboratory, whose Geophysics Directorate is located at Hanscom Air Force Base, Massachusetts, and two Navy organizations in the District of Columbia: the Office of Naval Research (ONR) and the Naval Research Laboratory (NRL). Although HAARP is funded through the DOD, civilian and university researchers have conducted research using the system.

The HAARP complex consists of 180 antenna towers configured in a grid of 15 columns and 12 rows spread across 58 acres of Alaskan wilderness land. The system is capable of transmitting 3.6 million watts of RF power and has a patented method for combining the energy in a focal beam array that is 72,000 times more powerful than the largest commercial radio station in the United States. Construction was completed, although the antennae array is scalable in the event more power is needed, in the year 2002. Antennae dipoles can operate in various frequency ranges [84]. Figure 14 depicts the HAARP antenna array from an aerial viewpoint..

Figure 14: HAARP Antenna Array

The HAARP project has configured an array of transmitters that emit sufficient signal strength to turn the aurora borealis into a virtual antenna, re-broadcasting in the extreme low frequency (ELF) range. Note that the ELF frequency range 6-10 Hz had been shown by David S. Walonick in his article "Effects of 6-10Hz ELF on Brain Waves" to have an effect on humans at the cellular level. EEG readings for the human brain operate in the range 0-20Hz or so. Thus, broadcasting using the HAARP antenna array minimally coincides with the biological frequency occurring in the human brain. What could a nation or army do with such a system? Imagine being able use HAARP as a weapon to broadcast with sufficient energy and in the proper frequency range, targeting opposing forces, cities, or entire continents. Given the sponsorship by the department of defense, who owns the land and sponsors the program,

HAARP used as a weapons has the ability to "fry" a human brain, much like the ultra-high-frequency antennas mounted on modern military vehicles and aircraft can do today. The system works by directing a transmitted ELF signal into the reflective ionosphere and bouncing the signal back to earth.

During active ionospheric research, the signal generated by the transmitter system is delivered to the antenna array, transmitted in an upward direction, and is partially absorbed, at an altitude between 100 to 350 km (depending on operating frequency), in a small volume a few hundred meters thick and a few tens of kilometers in diameter over the site. The intensity of the HF signal in the ionosphere is less than 3 microwatts per cm^2, tens of thousands of times less than the Sun's natural electromagnetic radiation reaching the earth and hundreds of times less than even the normal random *variations* in intensity of the Sun's natural ultraviolet (UV) energy which creates the ionosphere. The small effects that are produced, however, can be observed with the sensitive scientific instruments installed at the HAARP facility and these observations can provide new information about the dynamics of plasmas and new insight into the processes of solar-terrestrial interactions [84, 85].

Since October 1976, the former Union of Soviet Socialist Republics has been emitting ELF signals from Tesla-type transmitters. Source frequencies coincide exactly with brain-wave rhythms that have been shown to cause depression and irritability in humans. The signals emanating from Russia have been analyzed by the EPA and found to produce psychological-psychoactive responses in humans. The same ELF signals were also shown to be absorbed and re-radiated by 60Hz power transmission wires among other structures common to industrialized nations[85]. The point being that brain entrainment is known to occur as a result of external stimulation by electro-magnetic means, subsequently changing the brain waves to synchronize with the source ELF signal. The entrainment response causes changes in brain waves leading to altered chemistry and subsequent alteration in thoughts, emotions, and physical conditions. This is the basic mechanism by which an individual or population can be subjected to intra-cerebral mind control [85].

Various control and enslavement methods have been introduced in this chapter that is designed by governments to control their subjects. Methods ranging from chemical dependency, economic enslavement, structural disintegration, and active tampering with mental functions using external frequency entrainment all operate in coincidence to suppress human consciousness perpetuated by the ruling class. Humans for the most part are unwary victims of the degree to which they have been controlled while at the same time purported to have freedom but in fact it is basically an illusion.

9 THE WINGED-DISC GOD OF ZOROASTER

In the eastern part of ancient Persia over a thousand years BCE a religious philosopher named Zoroaster simplified the pantheon of early Iranian gods into two opposing forces: Ahura Mazda (Illuminating Wisdom) and Angra Mainyu (Destructive Spirit) which were in conflict.

Zoroaster's ideas led to a formal religion bearing his name by about the 6th century BCE and have influenced other later religions including Judaism, Gnosticism, Christianity and Islam.

Ancient inscriptions on the cliffs of Behistun in modern day Iran, are shown in Figure 15 depicting the deity Ahura Mazda flying in his winged-disc over king Darius I. This is the same symbol used by Enki in the flying disc symbol on the old Persian capital of Persepolis.

Figure 15: Behistun Inscription

According to Wikipedia sources, the inscription was authored by Darius the Great sometime between his coronation as king of the Persian Empire in the summer of 522 BC and his death in autumn of 486 BC. The inscription begins with a brief autobiography of Darius, including his ancestry and lineage. Later in the inscription, Darius provides a lengthy sequence of events following the deaths of Cyrus the Great and Cambyses II in which he fought nineteen battles in a period of one year (ending in December 521 BC) to put down multiple rebellions throughout the Persian Empire. The inscription states in detail that the rebellions, which had resulted from the deaths of Cyrus the Great and his son Cambyses II, were orchestrated by several impostors and their co-conspirators in various cities throughout the empire, each of whom falsely proclaimed kinghood during the upheaval following Cyrus's death. Darius the Great proclaimed himself victorious in all battles during the period of upheaval, attributing his success to the "grace of Ahura Mazda".

According to the tenets of the Zoroastrian religion, Ahura Mazda was the creator god of light and wisdom, and his arch rival, the creator of all destruction, was denoted as the god Angra Mainyu. It should not surprise the reader to know that Ahura Mazda was none other than Enki, and his half-brother Enlil played the role of the great destroyer, the precursor of the Christian devil, Angra Mainyu. If true, then the wiles of the Christian devil, promoted himself as God and demonized the true creator, Ahura Mazda, as Satan or a sneaky snake as evidenced in the later Biblical Canon.

Zoroastrianism, in various forms, served as the national or state religion for a large portion of the Iranian people for centuries. The religion began to fade when the Achaemenid Empire was invaded by Alexander the Great, subsequently disintegrating and was further marginalized by Islam from the 7th century onwards with the decline of the Sassanid Empire. It was at this juncture in history that Allah's Islam replaces Ahura Mazda's Zoroastrianism as the new state religion in Persia.

Given that the Mesopotamian territory had been allotted to Enlil, it was just a matter of time until the Enlilites routed the remnants of their nemesis Enkiites from the region. As evidenced by the situation in the Middle East, the Enlilites are growing in strength under the crescent moon-adorned flags in countries like Iran, Turkey, and Syria to name a few.

Babylon had a brief late flowering of power and influence under the Chaldean Dynasty which took over much of the empire formerly held by their northern kinsmen. However, the last king of Babylon, the Assyrian born Nabonidus, paid little attention to politics, preferring to obsess with worship of the moon god, leaving day to day rule to his son Belshazzar.

Could Allah, the god of the crescent moon, be none other than Nannar Sin, Enlil's son, as we have postulated herein? Since the Mesopotamian territory belonged to Enlil, his offspring, including the mood god Nannar, would have been welcomed there. Nannar was also a member of the Anunnaki council of 3760 BCE, and, as evidenced in the Atrahasis, he is shown to be the one that leads the Igigi miner's rebellion in Africa under Enlil's supervision.

There are links in historical texts indicating that Nannar-Sin had a very large following in his cult centers that were prolific in the area from southern Iraq to Syria, Turkey and Iran. Interestingly enough, the Kaba stone in Mecca, Saudi Arabia, one of the sacred centers for the religion of Islam, was originally dedicated to the moon god, referred to there as Allah. Could Nannar-Sin be the deity that Mohammed had an encounter with in the wilderness? Is Nannar-Sin the fabled Allah? Recall from the Atrahasis account:

Atrahasis Tablet 1 [37, pg 10]

Then **Alla** made his voice heard,

And spoke to the gods his brothers

Come! Let us carry Ellil,

The counselor of gods, the warrior, from his dwelling.

Now, cry battle!

The gods listened to his speech,

Set fire to their tools,

Put aside their spade for fire,

Their loads for the fire-god.

They flared up...

The author asserts that it is no coincidence that Alla(h) is leading the rebellion, right to his father Enlil's domicile. Note the fiery rhetoric he used to stir up the crowd of Igigi miners. Seems to me that his behavior is similar to that seen among the followers of Jihad in the Middle East, with spiritual leaders promoting warlike activities from the followers affiliated with the moon god, Allah.

The genealogy tables and Sumerian records clearly indicate that Enlil had a son on the Anunnaki council, Nannar Sin. Nannar (also called Sin) was the moon god; son of Enlil and Ninlil; father of Utu (sun god) and Inanna. It is not the intention of this book to definitively prove that the Alla referred to in the Atrahasis is the same Allah worshiped by Islam today, but would certainly be a terrific research project for those inclined toward finding the truth. How would the results of such research be received today? Knowing that Enlil was the god of Abraham, Isaac, and Jacob, the genocidal exterminator of early Mesopotamian slaves and the Great Flood Proponent devised to wipe out all flesh, changed my perspective on the many labels of "God". Hopefully, divulging the fact that Allah was an ancient astronaut from Nibiru and was the son of Enlil (AKA Zeus, Jupiter, Jehovah, El Shaddai...), will help illuminate the masses affiliated with the religion of the crescent moon.

Enlil's offspring invariably invade and overtake the colonies of Enki as happened in Atlantis and Mesopotamia. Thus Atlantis, a hidden away island, is still susceptible to the nautical Enlil pirates that invaded from their island base of Crete. Note that the pirates of Crete were similar to the roaming marauders that Enlil sponsored in Egypt, where their Biblical

Exodus story is severely mischaracterized. Keep in mind that Enlil was operating from the Levantine and Enki had his Egyptian domain adjacent to the headwaters of the Nile river delta, in North Africa.

Enki Establishes Atlantis

Speaking of Atlantis, we find a connection from Sumeria to Greece via this legendary lost city. We have written records about Atlantis recorded in the Timaeus by Plato. In the dialog between Critias and Socrates, a strange tale is conveyed which originated with Solon, wisest of the seven sages, although specified as true, regarding the Great Athenians, whose memory had passed into oblivion. Critias picks the most monumental story recorded by Solon's research, as a gratuity, stating that if Solon had finished the tale he would have been as famous as Homer [114, pg 26].

Critias continues, telling Socrates that at the head of the Egyptian delta, where the river Nile divides, there is a certain district which is called the district of Sais, and the great city of the district is also called Sais, and is the city from which sprang Amasis the king. And the citizens have a deity who is their foundress, called *Neith*, or *Athena* to the Greeks. Thus, the Egyptians felt a kindred connection to the Athenians. See God table 9.

Solon visited the Egyptian priests to find out what they knew about Greek history, the times of old, admitting that "neither he nor any other Greek new anything worth mentioning about the past." The reason the Greek history was lost was due to one of many destructions of mankind, arising out of varied causes. Further adding insult to a short Greek memory, the Egyptian priest from the Sais chastens Solon:

"As for those genealogies of yours which you have recounted to us Solon, they are no better than the tales of children, for in the first place, you remember one deluge only, where there were four with many lesser ones. In the next place, you do not know that there were dwelling in this land of yours one of the noblest races ever to have lived of whom your land and your people are only a remnant."

(gap)

"There was a time Solon, before the great deluge, when the city of Athens was the first in war and was preeminent for the excellence of her laws, and is said to have performed the noblest deeds and have the fairest constitutions of any which history tells upon the earth." [114, page 26]

Plato inherited the writings of Socrates, discussing the history of Greece in his unfinished notes. Solon, who was intending to use the tale of his poem involving the meaning of the historic Greek names provided by the Egyptian priests, detailing his country's noble ancestry. Plato picks up the lengthy tale, beginning with the assumption that the gods had divided the whole earth amongst themselves, subsequently building temples in which they were enthroned as gods, accepting sacrifices and offerings from the genetic underlings. Poseidon, the god of the sea, receiving for his lot the island of Atlantis.

According to the tale, Enki-Poseidon has children by a mortal woman, populating the island. In the account, a primitive man named Euenor lived in the surrounding mountains. Cleito, his daughter, caught Enki's fertility god eye. Poseidon fell in love with her, and had intercourse with her and, breaking the ground, enclosed the hill in which she dwelt all round, making alternate zones of sea and land, larger and smaller, encircling one another.

Enki begat and brought up five pairs of male children, dividing the island of Atlantis into ten portions; he gave to his first born of the eldest pair, his mother's dwelling and the surround allotment, which was the largest and best, and made him king over the rest; the others he made princes, and gave them rule over many men and a large territory. He named them all. The eldest who was king, he named Atlas, and from him the whole island and the ocean received its name [114, pg 39]. Extensive details about all aspects of Atlantis are provided by Plato's writing, recounting Solons historical foray into the discovery of their noble links to the past. Thus, the mystery of Greek history was spelled out for Solon, and relayed to the world by Plato. This accounting has been the factual basis for the search for Atlantis for many years, continuing to this day. Based on the writings, it seems obvious that the island city of Atlantis was located along the rim of the now submerged Atlas Mountain range in Northern Africa.

Without the aid of a bronze age map depicting the port cities of the world, one could not rebuff the Darwinists who believed the sea levels circa 2000 B.C. were little different than today. Yet the presence of hundreds of submerged ancient construction sites from the Gulf of Chambay to Bimini, and from Cornwall to Nan Madol, certainly contradict that notion. Most of the submerged ruins worldwide are situated in the Mediterranean and eastern Atlantic, right where you'd expect them to be, where king Atlas plied the waters, building port facilities as told in Solon's tale, now submerged since the end of the last Ice Age.

Critias by Plato [114, pg 32]

For many generations, as long as the divine natured lasted in them, they were obedient to the laws and well affectioned towards the gods who were their kinsmen, for they possessed true and in every way great spirits, practicing gentleness and wisdom in the various changes of life, and in their intercourse with one another. They despised everything but virtue, nor caring for their present state of life, and thinking lightly on the possession of gold and other property which seemed only a burden to them. Neither were they intoxicated by luxury, nor did wealth deprive them of their self-control, but they were sober and saw clearly all these goods were increased by virtuous friendship with one another, and that by excessive zeal for them, and honor of them, the good of them is lost, and friendship perishes with them."

We have traced a few of the complex civilizations that Enki was involve in launching, from Eridu to Persia, Atlantis, Egypt and Greece. Next we will explore the Anunnaki lessons taught to us about the Heavens.

10 CELESTIAL TIME AND ZODIAC RULERS

Living in the big city is hardly conducive to a successful hobby in astronomy. Cities near the coast are often overcast given the formulation of a marine layer. This moisture, coupled with prolific artificial lighting emanating from landscape and security lights, among a multitude of others, effectively blocks one's ability to see the stars at night. Vacating the city and driving inland to unpopulated areas, ideally at altitude and sporting low humidity on a cloudless partial moon-lit evening is where you will find the stargazers.

Imaging living in a situation where one spent 3-4 hours a day doing the domestic chore of securing resources needed to survive, then being in nature enjoying life without corporate enslavement, as Zog the caveman lived. Okay, my virtual vacation aside, the stargazers of the past somehow, either of their own accord or with alien help, mapped the stars, grouped them into a suspiciously but profound twelve symbols still in use today. They also built sophisticated temples using the megalithic stone blocks which tracked changes in the precessional slip the earth exhibits due to a wobble in its inclined rotational axis. This detailed level of knowledge is impressive.

Consider Zog, the hypothetical caveman with a nerdy disposition, who decides to make a mark on a stone where a shadow is cast at first light each day, and being a truly dedicated observer, continues his markings on the rock for at least one full solar cycle (365 days). Zog would have data to show that on a certain day the cycle repeated, perhaps he would have been keen enough to pick an unusual day, like the longest or shortest day as his focal point for the analysis. This implies that Zog would also have to have kept track of the length of the day to assess which day is the longest or shortest. In either event, assuming a lot here, one could notice that the initial mark made on the stone at the shadow's edge would not line up with the mark made on the same day one solar cycle ago. This is where one would need the knowledge of the division of a circle into some number of finite divisions. The concept of a circle, the Earth rotating on an inclined angle with an induced wobble, with precession relative to the solar ecliptic experiencing slippage at a rate that enabled long-term calendar event planning, are difficult to fathom that Zog figured out on all this requisite knowledge through his own through observations. Turns out that using three hundred and sixty degrees as the segmented measure allows one to represent the rotational pattern of the earth around the sun, in a convenient mathematical form that also allows application of the constant π to Volume, Circumference, and Area measurements of a circle.

Could the stargazing cave nerd have been smart enough to have specified a unique day from which to compare the assumed repeating data cycles? If the 360 degree division standard was adopted and used, then we would find that the difference in the first mark on the stone and the one that is a full solar cycle away, namely 364.25 days, round to 365, would be $1/72^{nd}$ of a degree offset. Thus, Zog would have to extrapolate to figure out that it would take 72 full solar cycles to offset the mark on the stone by

1 degree, having dividing the circle arbitrarily into 360 degrees with a lucky guess. Thus, for the shadow mark etched on the "marker stone" to travel a full circle and arrive back at the same point as that annotated the first year, would take 72 years times 360 degrees, or 25,920 years. That's a lot of shells and beads to represent a "Great Year" as it is termed [20.]

This is the level of knowledge that would be needed to begin to comprehend the scientific basis for the earth's processional movement around the solar ecliptic. Why would one dedicate such significant time observing the movements of the sun on the horizon? Unless of course you were a nerd like Zog, or more likely a temple priest watching the heavens for the appointed time of change to be communicated to the next Zodiac ruler, in preparation for a change in command. For the record, occurring on 07.29.13 as I work on this book, the Grand Sextile Alignment is occurring, creating a Star of David in the Heavens, for the 13th time since 1990 is truly significant as a War Star sign. There is a lot of buzz on YouTube about this event as the next one will not occur for over 100 years from now. Is it a coincidence, that simultaneously, Israel just bombed Damascus, again, as the world awaits a response? The situation in Syria appears to be a Biblically significant war, especially if Damascus becomes a ruinous heap as Isaiah 17:1 predicts it will as part of the end times.

Farmers have used the knowledge of the longest day of winter as a marker point in the planting cycle, seeking the earliest time in the season, depending on geography, to sew their crops averting a crop damaging frost. The coming of the Spring Equinox was celebrated around the ancient world. Recognition of this event was fashioned in the temple architecture, providing a long axis aligned to the point on the earth's horizon where the sun rises, channeling the sunlight along a corridor with a marker stone to save the place where the light strikes. To make the measurement relevant, the designer had to keep in mind that the earth is precessing, moving opposite the direction of rotation.

Thus, the marks on the stone where the sun struck would be moving as indicated previously for Zog. An ingenious way to deal with this is to assign the 360 degree circle representing the orbital path with a set of divisions which can be visually tracked in the night sky. This is where the twelve houses of the Zodiac, provided to the Sumerians by the Anunnaki, are so useful. Simply using the star groupings relative to the horizon, split into three slices: Southern Hemisphere, Northern Hemisphere, and the Central Zone along the earth's equator. Interestingly enough, the three segments were assigned to Enki, Enlil, and Anu respectively.

At this point in our pretend scenario, assuming Zog would have been able to simply watch the night sky and put together the Zodiac House we still use today is questionable. That said, the Anunnaki not only divulged this knowledge to the Sumerians, they even had their namesakes affiliated with the planets as shown in Table 6 below.

Anunnaki	Planetary Affiliation	Symbol
Anu	Uranus	♅
Enlil	Jupiter	♃
Enki	Neptune	♆

Ningishzida	Mercury	☿
Inanna	Venus	♀
Iskur-Adad	Mars	♂

Table 6: Anunnaki Planetary Affiliation

It is interesting times we are living in as it relates to astronomy. Pluto was recently demoted from planetary status and the thirteenth sign of Ophiuchus was added to the official Zodiac as of the year 2011. According to Robert Brit, Senior Science writer for Space.com, capping years of intense debate, astronomers resolved on August 24th, 2006, to demote Pluto from planetary status to a dwarf planet category. Was this done as an appeasement to the Mayan predictions? The reason is unclear.

The hidden sign of Ophiuchus was designated between Sagittarius and Scorpio. It was stated in Mayan legends that the point in celestial time that the Sun would rise in the sign of Ophiuchus coincides with the solar system's passage through the galactic center [66,67].

By the 1930's, the astronomical community had accepted the fact that the Galactic Center was located in the constellation of Sagittarius. Early observations studying the source of static that was affecting transatlantic phone calls, led to the discovery of a 20.5 MHz frequency being emitted in the constellation of Sagittarius, then known to be Galactic Center by scientists. The theory of the existence of a black hole at the center of our galaxy was put forth by Martin Rees and Donald Lynden-Bell in 1971. They believed that a black hole could be one possible explanation for the tremendous amount of energy that had been detected coming from the Galactic Center [109].

Just three years later, Bruce Balick and Robert Brown detected such a compact source in the inner one parsec core of the galactic nucleus [109]. They found the location of this extremely energetic source, Sagittarius A star, to coincide with the dynamical center of the galaxy. The scientists had detected the first evidence that a massive black hole resided in the heart of our galaxy. The exact distance from the Sun to the Galactic Center falls within the range 25,000 to 28,000 light years away. Due to the presence of interstellar dust, the Galactic Center cannot be studies in the visible, ultraviolet or X-ray wavelengths. Current scientific data comes from observations using gamma rays, infrared, hard X-rays, and sub-millimeter radio wavelengths.

The Milky Way passes through about 30 constellations. The band divides the night sky into two roughly equal hemispheres. The Galactic plane is inclined by about 60 degrees to the plane of the Earth's orbit. Why would one care about the center of the galaxy? Modern science, studying solar system physics, has shown that the radiation within the galactic center is much higher than outside that plane. Staying away from the galactic center has an additional advantage. The center of the Galaxy is awash in harmful radiation. Solar systems near the center would experience increased exposure to gamma rays, X-rays, and cosmic rays, which would destroy any life trying to evolve on a planet.

Radiation is measured in micro Sieverts, designated by μSv. The average radiation you receive per day is about 10 μSv. Visiting the dentist for an X-ray radiates you with 100 μSv, ten times the normal amount received in a day. The maximum allowable radiation dose for humans in the United States, for occupational standards, is 50,000 μSv. Severe radiation poisoning occurs at 2 million μSv and 6-8 million μSv causes death. The Milky Way's Galactic Cosmic Radiation, or GCR, is found between a few tenths and few tens of GeV (yes, 10 Giga Electron Volts). exceeding deadly human exposure limits.

Referencing an article found online [118], in which the astronomer Parke Kunkle wrote for NBC news, he states that due to the Earth's changing alignment in the last 3000 years, the sign you were born into is now different than it was long ago. Additionally, a 13th Zodiac sign called Ophiuchus, which falls between Scorpio and Sagittarius, should amend the existing twelve (12) signs...

"This is not something that happened today. This has gone on for thousands of years," says Kunkle. " Because of this change of tilt, the Earth is really over here in effect and Sun is in a different constellation than it was 3,000 years ago."

The constellation of Ophiuchus is located near the celestial equator and is typically depicted as a man wrangling a serpent. "Ophiuchus" means "serpent-bearer" in Greek. One of several different characters from Greek mythology that Ophiuchus was thought to represent was Asclepius the healer. The snake is often associated with doctors, thanks to Thoth's Caduceus, so Ophiuchus is often associated with healing images. The

Romans also associated the constellation with Asclepius, who learned the secret to immortality by watching one serpent treat another serpent with healing herbs. Zeus summarily killed Asclepius with a lightning bolt because he didn't want everyone to be immortal, but later honored his good deeds by giving him a spot in the heavens. Sounds like something Enlil would do.

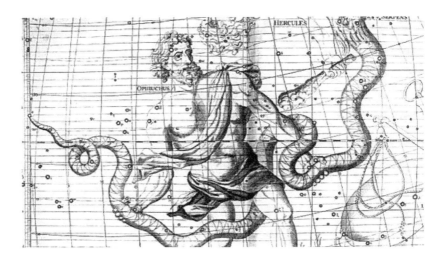

Figure 16: Ophiuchus, the Missing Zodiac Sign

This story sounds just like the god of wrath and vengeance given his bad behavior in Mesopotamia, i.e. the consciousness-suppressing activities Enlil exhibits from the Atrahasis account forward in his relationship to mankind.

The sign Ophiuchus can be found in the Sidereal Zodiac used by Hindu astrologers. The Sidereal Zodiac's astrological sign dates are based on a moving Zodiac which has shifted almost one full sign from the fixed zodiac with 12 signs still in use today. Thus, modern stargazers should technically be using these dates, shown below, which reflect the current alignment of the Sun, Earth and stars augmented with the missing sign of Ophiuchus.

Zodiac Sign	Date Range
Capricorn	Jan. 20 - Feb. 16
Aquarius	Feb. 16 - March 11
Pisces	March 11- April 18
Aries	April 18- May 13
Taurus	May 13- June 21
Gemini	June 21- July 20
Cancer	July 20- Aug. 10
Leo	Aug. 10- Sept. 16
Virgo	Sept. 16- Oct. 30
Libra	Oct. 30- Nov. 23
Scorpio	Nov. 23- Nov. 29
Ophiuchus	Nov. 29- Dec. 17
Sagittarius	Dec. 17- Jan. 20

Table 7: Amended Thirteenth Zodiac Sign

Each Zodiac sign is provided with a slice of the 360 degree circle. There are different models, some which divide the twelve signs evenly provisioning thirty degrees per sign. Others allocate different degrees to each sign based its actual transit time. Thus, using this method, not all Zodiac signs have the same duration [45]. The Anunnaki relied on the accurate time-keeping priests and temple calendars to observe the heavens and track the precessional sign the earth was in. Temples aligned either to equinox or solstice points on the Eastern horizon, often had segmented viewing regions partitioned into either equivalent Zodiac house models, implying thirty degrees for each house, or unequal viewing segments based on their measured degrees in the specific Zodiac sign. Temples in use that exceeded the viewing azimuth for a given Zodiacal house, were sometimes re-oriented along a new viewing axis. This costly oversight would have led to a more circular design structure like that used in Stone Henge, allowing the architecture to adapt to the moving processional azimuths.

Archeoastronomy is a new science that takes into account the building alignment as a function of which Zodiacal house the sun would be rising in during that time period. Using this method has helped archeologists date stone structures that may be devoid of carbon-datable material [115]. Wikipedia has a nice write up on the subject for those inclined to try it using software.

Rulership was an important part of the transfer of kingship from Nibiru to Earth. The Sumerian King's list provides a detailed, yet hard to believe record that dates back over 400,000 years ago. Given the ready affiliation of the Anunnaki namesakes with the known planets in our solar system, it should come as no surprise that the method chosen to justify a change in rulership, or whether it was simply agreed upon that when the Zodiac House changes, the jockeying for power and position on the Council of Twelve rose to saber rattling intensity levels. *Consider our current Age change from Pisces to Aquarius, council change time!!!*

From the "Wars of Gods and Men", Sitchin describes a scenario in which Marduk makes a power grab approximately 24 years too early. The ability to accurately measure which Zodiacal house the sun was rising in was critical to those in power. Affiliating namesakes with planets was the ultimate power play. The following table shows the planets, their distance from the sun, and the solar orbital period in days. The information for Nibiru is not available (yet), although the orbital period was clearly specified as 3,600 Earth years. See Table 8.

Planet	Distance from Sun (million km)	Mass of Planet ($\times 10^{22}$kg)	Solar Orbital Time Days
Mercury	58	33.00	88.0
Venus	108	487.00	224.7
Earth	150	598.00	365.2
Mars	228	64.20	687.0
Jupiter	778	190,000	4,332
Saturn	1,429	56,900	10760
Uranus	2871	8,690	30,700
Neptune	4,504	10,280	60,200
Pluto	5,913	1.49	90,600
Nibiru	5,913+ ??	???	1,314,720

Table 8: Planetary Orbital Table

Several authors have pointed out the use of the Golden Mean Rectangle in various temples designs around the world. Recall that the fractional number of 1.618 has been declared the divine creation ratio, or Φ (Phi), It is derived from examining the Fibonacci Sequence which specifies the design ratio that also shows up in the heavens. The sequence is:

1,1,2,3,5,8,13,21,34,55...n=(n-1+n-2)

The Φ ratio is derived by dividing a number in the sequence by its n-1 antecedent. Do this enough times and you will see the ratio converges to 1.618, rather quickly.

$$1/1=1$$
$$2/1=2$$
$$3/2=1.50$$
$$5/3=1.66$$
$$8/5=1.60$$
$$13/8=1.625$$
$$21/13=1.615$$
$$34/21=1.619$$
$$55/34=1.618$$

As you can see the series converges to 1.618 while oscillating around the Φ like a damped sinusoid before converging to the creator's assumed design ratio. Also, of great interest, is finding this same ratio between the Earth and Venus. Dividing the solar orbital period of Earth by that of Venus, and you find the same ratio, Φ. As above, so below it seems. Was this planetary ratio between Earth and Venus, also found in a plethora of terrestrial plants and animals to include humans, an intentional artifact left over by the creator of the solar system, perhaps the Creator of All's handiwork, as alluded to by the Anunnaki themselves?

Thoth, as we know was none other than Enki's son Ningishzida. He wrote the Emerald Tablets, in which he describes building the Giza pyramid structure. From the first tablet, he states:

Emerald Tablets, Introduction [76]

When Thoth, *the Atlantean and Master* raised the people of Khem (Egypt) to a great civilization. and when the time came for him to leave Egypt, he erected The Great Pyramid over the entrance of the *Great Halls of Amenti*. In the Pyramid, he posited his records and appointed Guards for his secrets from among the highest of his people.

In later times. the descendants of these guards became the Pyramid Priests, while *Thoth* was deified as the God of Wisdom, the Recorder, by those in the age of darkness which followed his passing. In legend, the Halls of Amenti became the underworld, the *Halls of the Gods*, where the soul passed after death for judgment.

According to modern researchers, the pyramids of Giza were constructed during the Age of Leo, which began in 10,500 BCE and lasted until 8,000 BCE. Thus the Sphinx has the body of a lion, the Zodiac sign of Leo, and the face of Thoth its builder, as stated in the Emerald Tablets. Sitchin also reports the same data from his records, giving credit to Thoth for the "building that is like a mountain" construction. David Hatcher Childress, world explorer and author, regularly conducts Giza plateau Egypt tours as well as in South America, another Anunnaki mining outpost. See http://davidhatcherchildress.com for more details.

Without getting to far off the mark, while serving as a Chief Warrant Officer and Attack helicopter pilot in the U.S. Army 1982-1989, the concept of gyroscopic precession lay at the technical basis for why a rotorcraft operated the way it did, as taught in Flight School, Fort Rucker, Alabama, graduating Light Blue Flight class of 85-13. I digress. The angular momentum conserving principle states that applying a stimulus to a rotating body will manifest the input force offset by ninety degrees in the direction of rotation. This is interesting helicopter feature, to see the helicopter's rotating swashplate tilt to the right given the counter clockwise blade rotation, as the cyclic control input is straight ahead, causing the aircraft to fly straight forward as a result of this phenomenon.

Now consider the Earth rotating like a gyroscope, the likes of which one finds in a toy store. If the top of the toy were split into two equal halves of a circle, letting one half be black and the other red, then an interesting visual effect can be observed. While the top is spinning perfectly straight up and down, the two halves of the circles will appear to stay stationary, differentiating the red and the black colored semi-circles clearly.

Now, introduce a slight wobble to the stable spinning gyroscope by tapping it with your finger. Observe the colored circles looking directly from above. You will see that the semi-circles appear to be rotating in the opposite direction of rotation. The slight wobble introduced causes the vertical axis to slip due to the coefficient of friction increase which occurs where the surface area of the top impacts the horizontal support surface. As the top slows down, with the angular momentum forces decreasing, the wobble is exaggerated.

At various rotational speeds, the wobbling toy will skip, coincident with where the point of impact was first imparted to the top. One can think of this induced wobble as an analogous event that must have occurred in the heavens such that the Earth has an inclined orbit of approximately 23.5 degrees relative to the solar ecliptic. Is it possible that the source of the Earth's wobble is some event that coincides with the Great Year? The implication would be that some force acting on the Earth was significant enough to cause the planet to tilt away from the expected solar plane. An space intruder like a comet, asteroid, planet, or meteor could be the source of the Earth's tilt and potentially the wobble as well. Another speculative possibility for the reader to consider is that the forces within the Galactic Center could be responsible to some degree for the Earth's cyclical perturbations alluded to by the Mayans.

Consider the 60 degree tilted plane our solar system has relative to the Galactic Center plane. If our entire solar system were to pass through the Milky Way Galaxy center in the sign of Ophiuchus as the Mayans stated, then every 13,000 years or so our entire solar system would cross through the highly radiated Galactic Center being exposed to an intense gravity field.

Try spinning a bicycle wheel in your hands, feeling the angular momentum forces by changing the spin axis orientation. The spinning gyroscope will oppose changes in the rotational plane. Now orient the spinning tire 60 degrees relative to the ceiling, representing the Galactic Center as a force field. The force of gravity within the plane is much higher than outside, evidenced by the flat spinning, disk shaped geometry evidenced by images taken by the Hubble Telescope. If the spinning bike tire strike the ceiling at a 60 degree angle, lifting it with your hands, what happens? Due to gyroscopic precession previously discussed, the impact force of the ceiling, simulating the gradient field effect imposed by the massive black hole gravity flux, would show up ninety degrees in the direction of rotation causing the Earth to potentially flip and rotate about its axis, possibly explaining the plate techtonic sudden shift theory that Charles Hapgood wrote about in his book, supported by Einstein in 1953.

Einstein commented on Hapgood's theory, stating that in a polar region there is continual deposition of ice, which is not symmetrically distributed about the pole. The earth's rotation acts on these asymmetrically deposited masses, and produces centrifugal momentum that is transmitted to the rigid crust of the earth. The constantly increasing centrifugal momentum produced in this way will, when it has reached a certain point, produces a movement of the earth's crust over the rest of the earth's body... [108].

The Anunnaki imparted to mankind significant knowledge about the workings in the heavens, planetary orbits and interactions having formed the basis of the Enuma Elish, their creation account. Enoch was taken aloft by the Anunnaki and taught the entire workings of the heavens [36]. Advanced knowledge about the long wobble witnessed in the Earth's processional movements, allowed the Niburian astronauts to create an ingenious system of Zodiac Houses assigned to a twelve, or thirteen part wheel, if including the recently added sign of Orphiuchus, thereby establishing a mechanism for term limits and power sharing by the elite.

Temples were built aligned to the compass points in order to accurately assess the repeating cycles of time. With the Zodiac Age changes came restructuring among the Anunnaki rulers. All one needed to know was that every 72 years a 1 degree slip occurs in the Zodiac wheel. If each of the original twelve houses of the Zodiac were equivalent, namely 30 degrees, then each sign would last 72 years times 30 degrees equaling 2,160 years. So, approximately every two thousand years, major changes took place in leadership, often times impacting mankind with memorable events and wars [18]...

11 WARRING FACTIONS PAST AND PRESENT

Given the rivalry that began to build among the Anunnaki deities over occupied lands, specifically between archrivals Enlil and Enki; Anu scheduled a political visit to arbitrate the conflict. The year was 3760 BCE according to the Sumerian records, and the destination was the Sumerian city of Uruk, the city of King Gilgamesh. Cuneiform records detail the visit in intricate detail. The practical aspects of the trip involved specifically segregating the targeted regions for Anu's direct reports and their offspring.

The four regions the Anunnaki identified in the records were: the Sinai Peninsula, Mesopotamia, Egypt and South Africa, and the Indus Valley. Enki got the African continent. Marduk remained in his Gateway of the Gods City of Babylon, clearly violating the terms of the territorial segregation having given Mesopotamia to Enlil, as Lord of the Command. Enki's offspring were expected to move to live within the protection provided in Africa, appears to be the implication which Marduk rejected. This created conflicts, which escalated and eventually led to wars. The incursion on the rival brother's territory, you will recall from the Atrahasis account, is the reason given by Noah to leave Shurrupak, claiming that Enlil no longer found favor with him and that he would need to move to Africa, Enki's domain, to avoid conflict.

Marduk maneuvers to avenge his father Enki which subsequently leads to war with Ninurta over Zodiac timing. Conflicting accuracy of solar versus solar-lunar calendars, as implemented by Thoth in the Yucatan, starting August 11, 3114 BCE, triggered the war. This is the Mayan long count start date. Using both the solar and lunar cycle data provided Thoth with a more accurate calendar, one which could help avoid confusion over Zodiacal house boundaries, subsequently averting skirmishes among the current and upcoming heirs to the Niburian allotted throne. Chichin Itza, the temple of the moon and the sun, is an example of the advanced timekeeping structures built in the Yucatan Peninsula, as eloquently detailed by Sitchin in his book "The Lost Realms" [19]

Biblical Canon and liturgical dogma often represent the covenant that Enlil makes with Abram, renaming him Abraham thereafter, to give his seed the land of Israel. Recall from Genesis:

Genesis 15:1-17 : The LORD's Covenant With Abram

1 After this, the word of the LORD came to Abram in a vision:

"Do not be afraid, Abram.
I am your shield,
your very great reward."

2 But Abram said, "Sovereign LORD, what can you give me since I remain childless and the one who will inherit my estate is Eliezer of

Damascus?" ³ And Abram said, "You have given me no children; so a servant in my household will be my heir."

⁴ Then the word of the LORD came to him: "This man will not be your heir, but a son who is your own flesh and blood will be your heir." ⁵ He took him outside and said, "Look up at the sky and count the stars— if indeed you can count them." Then he said to him, "So shall your offspring be."

⁶ Abram believed the LORD, and he credited it to him as righteousness.

⁷ He also said to him, "I am the LORD, who brought you out of Ur of the Chaldeans to give you this land to take possession of it."

(gap)

¹² As the sun was setting, Abram fell into a deep sleep, and a thick and dreadful darkness came over him. ¹³ Then the LORD said to him, "Know for certain that **for four hundred years your descendants** will be strangers in a country not their own and that they will be enslaved and mistreated there. ¹⁴ But I will punish the nation they serve as slaves, and afterward they will come out with great possessions. ¹⁵ You, however, will go to your ancestors in peace and be buried at a good old age. ¹⁶ In the fourth generation your descendants will come back here, for the sin of the Amorites has not yet reached its full measure."

¹⁷ When the sun had set and darkness had fallen, a smoking firepot with a blazing torch appeared and passed between the pieces. ¹⁸ On that day the LORD made a covenant with Abram and said, "To your descendants I give this land, from the Wadi of Egypt to the great river, the Euphrates— ¹⁹the land of the Kenites, Kenizzites, Kadmonites, ²⁰ Hittites, Perizzites, Rephaites, ²¹ Amorites, Canaanites, Girgashites and Jebusites."

As noted, the land that Abraham was to be given was already occupied by several different tribes to include the Hittites and the Canaanites. If a land is given to you but someone is already occupying the region, the gotcha is that Abraham and his successors would be ordered to conduct a genocidal incursion into the region, murdering all that lived in each village, until the entire area had been cleared. What kind of person would sign up to a real-estate deal like that?

Enlil made a covenant with Abram to route the existing occupants of the Levantine via his offspring, not him personally. This was tantamount to genocide, Enki's offspring were the targets. It is told in the Canonical bible from the Jacob standpoint. What about the Ishmael standpoint in the Qur'an [115]? After all, if a child is going to be sacrificed to God as an offering, abominable to consider in and of itself, why not sacrifice the one that was not in line to be heir, namely Ishmael? The Koran specifies that this was the child taken to Mount Horeb, not Jacob as told the Bible.

How does one ascribe the term "righteous", as Abram did in verse Genesis 15:6, to the LORD that made the deal with him, at the same time declaring that Abram himself will never make it to the land described in the covenant, but rather he would meet his ancestors first as stated in verse 15. *You, however, will go to your ancestors instead of benefitting from our deal.* Oh, your offspring will benefit though, after numerous wars based on Enlil's desire to exterminate any life in the Levantine.

This is one of many examples in which the brothers, or their offspring went to war. Mankind was merely a pawn in the territorial disputes that arose in the region. The skirmishes were not limited to direct conflicts between Enki and Enlil, but rather sprang up among their progeny as well. Enki and Marduk, the great Egyptian gods Ptah and Ra respectively, actively participated in the genetic wars against the Enlilites.

Enki produced prolific and strategic offspring at critical junctures in mankind's history. In the *Enki and Ninharsag* Paradise Myth, a strategic conjugal visit occurs in an attempt to spawn a rightful heir. After all, Ninharsag was Enki's half sister. In the tale, aspirations to control part of the Sinai peninsula that contained the relocated space port from Sippar, the Egyptian pyramids used for navigational and other means, were discussed between the two. Several children were born to Enki, but the offspring from Ninharsag ended up being a girl, disqualified from rulership. He kept trying, producing eight progeny, six females and two males resulted. Each offspring was assigned politically strategic roles designed to subvert, although subtly at times, Enlil's authority and command. Whoever controlled the space related facilities could access the space vehicles and communications equipment that was the Anunnaki's only link to their home planet, where critical resources traded hands.

Recall the tale of Isis, Osiris, and Horus from the land of Egypt. In the account, Seth left upper Egypt (south) to the coveted lower region (north) allotted to Horus. Seth eliminated Osiris using a deceitful coffin trick, and appeared to have gotten away with the murder until Horus is genetically reconstituted from the dead god's phallus (semen or DNA?) by Ninharsag (Isis). His rejoicing coup came to an end in the year 363 BCE when Horus takes revenge on Seth, starting what is termed the first Pyramid War. According to Sitchin, this is the first war that the gods used men as their expendable pawns. [18 pg 155].

Horus recruits other gods from Africa to counter attack the incursions of Seth. Aided by the Winged Disk that Thoth made, Horus made his way north toward the Giza plateau. According to the records, a significant skirmish took place near a chain of lakes separating the Sinai peninsula and Egypt. Much carnage ensued, Seth's forces suffering significant casualties. The war escalated to the point that Seth and Horus engaged in direct combat with each other. Their tactical escapades involve using tunnels for cover and concealment and aerial combat over the Sinai peninsula. Horus prevailed and the Anunnaki Council delegates the Egypt region to Horus as the victor. Seth was banished from the region, purportedly taking up domicile as an exile in eastern Asian island according to Sitchin.

Additional conflicts persisted between the Enlilites and Enkiites, strategically focused on controlling space related facilities like Giza, the space port in the Sinai, and mission control functions in Jerusalem.

Enlil won the Lord of the Command title to replace Enki in

Mesopotamia as predicated by Anu during his paternal referee visit circa 3760 BCE. Thus, the Jewish people, descendants of Jacob, were in a geographic position to be promoted as the guardians of the "portal" that was built beneath the Temple Mount in Jerusalem. This Anunnaki only portal was used for high-level VIP travelers that visited Earth from Nibiru like Anu. This was the post-dilluvial bond Heaven-Earth. Anu visited Earth using this portal, and various missions to Nibiru were launched from Jerusalem's mission control center [53]

According to the Qur'an, Mohammed was shuttled from Mecca to Jerusalem where he ascended to heaven [115]. It is the author's humble opinion that the portal of Mount Horeb, similar to the one found in Uruk, is the reason behind the world's obsession with Jerusalem. According to the Lost Book of Enoch, the watchers are to be punished at the end of days [36, pg 122]. These convicts on "death row" until that appointed time would definitely want a way out if one existed. The only way off the planet was via rocket ship, shem as they were deemed, or via the portal reserved for VIPs. Since the convicted rebels would most likely be restricted from accessing vehicles that provided them a ready Earth-prison break, the portal may have been the only Anunnaki bond heaven-earth space facility remnant left on Earth. Thus, protecting access to the portal, assuming it is still functional, would be of tantamount importance on Earth, as evidenced by the alliances and maneuverings between the United States and Israel relative to their perceived enemies.

What possible influences animate the leaders of such powerful countries? For those paying attention to the symbols used by the modern day kings and their affiliated kingdoms, the all seeing eye atop the partially completed pyramid, as designed into the world's standard currency, the U.S.

Dollar, begs the most casual observer to query the origins of such ancient trademarks. Could it be that the power behind the secret societies, such as the Masons and their infiltrators, the Illuminati, as documented by Laurence Gardener in his premier book "Genesis of the Grail Kings", are broadcasting their intent to establish a Novus Ordo Seclorum, a New World Order? The first phrase, Annuit Coeptis, is less well known in translation from Latin. According to Wikipedia, the phrase is taken from the Latin words *annuo*, *annuit* in its third person present perfect form, means to nod or approve. The term coeptum is translated as commencement or undertaking. Together the accepted translation is "He approved of the undertakings". There are implications that God (He) is the approving authority of the New World Order undertakings, although any label of "God" was left off the back of the dollar by the U.S Mint. See Figure 17 below.

Figure 17: World's Superpower Currency

The 1782 resolution adopting the seal blazons the image on the reverse as "A pyramid unfinished. In the zenith an eye in a triangle, surrounded by a glory, proper." The pyramid is conventionally shown as consisting of 13 layers to refer to the 13 original states. The adopting resolution provides that it is inscribed on its base with the date MDCCLXXVI (1776) in Roman numerals. Where the top of the pyramid should be, the Eye of Providence watches over it.

The Eye of Providence (or the all-seeing eye of God) is a symbol showing an eye often surrounded by rays of light or a glory and usually enclosed by a triangle. It is sometimes interpreted as representing the **eye of God** watching over humankind. Imagery of an all-seeing eye can be traced back to Egyptian mythology and the Eye of Horus, and is affiliated with Freemasonry today, as evidenced in the architecture of the "Great Temple" of the 33rd degree Scottish Rite Temple located in Washington D.C.

Figure 18: The Great Temple All-Seeing Eye

Note the triangle with rays of light emanating out of the center. While visiting Washington D.C. and the Library of Congress in the year 2009, doing research for this book, a private tour visit was arranged to see the insides of the Scottish Rite Temple, headquartered there. It was here that the theories I had been researching involving the Sumerians transformed from a curious delving into the past as a hobby, to a serious matter to contemplate. It was clearly evident that the Masons had played a pivotal role in the founding of the Washington, D.C., the new Atlantis where the trestleboard plans for a Novus Ordum Seclorum were memorialized on the nation's currency, lest one be in doubt as to the identity of the hidden, yet all powerful architects and purveyors of the New World Order [65].

Enoch describes his journey to Nibiru, although his departure location is unclear. Enoch is a central character to the Masonic rituals. He lived 365 years (symbolic of the days in a year?) and then was no more as he took up residence with "God".

Genesis 5:21 (NIV)

When Enoch had lived 65 years, he became the father of Methuselah. And after he became the father of Methuselah, Enoch walked with God 300 years and had other sons and daughters. Enoch walked with God; then he was no more, because God took him away.

The lost book of Enoch states that he was involved in playing an intercessionary role between higher level Anunnaki Council members and Azazael, the Igigi commander that led the 200 rebels to take human women for themselves. The end of days mentioned in the Book of Enoch implies that the Igigi remnants that broke galactic law knew that there was no escaping the punishment that was due. In the end times, they would be looking for a portal, like the one that once existed in Uruk, and likely exists beneath the temple mount in Jerusalem, to exit planet Earth and attempt to flee in exile. As the judgment date draws nearer, those alien astronauts condemned for their rebellious act to sew their genetic seed among man, will attempt all means to control access to Jerusalem's portal, using humans as expendable fodder in their quest to escape punishment.

The destruction of the Tower of Babylon was committed by Enlil and his son Ninurta, most likely, given the circumstances and the bloodline feud. Destroying the tower, most certainly a space vehicle launch facility, was wrought to avert Marduk, chief deity of Babylon and son of Enki, from bypassing the Sinai space port. The Sinai territory was under Ninharsag's authority, although Enlil treated it as his own. Therefore, Enlil decided to destroy Marduk's obvious attempt to grab power and authority in the region from the Enlilites by having his own bond heaven-Earth facilities, to come and go as he pleased without Enlil's control.

Marduk was termed "he of the pure mound" by his father Enki and had the added title of "Marduk the Avenger", implying a sworn oath to avenge his father for averted birth right issues whose origins apparently had their source back home on Nibiru [18]. This inheritance misunderstanding between the half-brothers was epic and played out over long periods of time on Earth, given the Anunnaki gods ability to master time, living for incredible durations although not impervious to death.

Consider the infamous hillbilly combatants, the Hatfields and McCoy's family feud; now add hundreds if not millions of years of evolutionary sophistication and technology, to include nuclear weapons and genetic engineering, and you then understand the historical setting. This alien bad behavior should be familiar to mankind, after all we have their genetic mark, and apparently their warring disposition as well, given fallen state of the world today. The world's nations are in warring chaos and the average person is contemplating whether these are the end of days? Israel is surrounded by hostile threats and Apocalyptic maneuvers are under way.

Marduk, having carved out the city of Babylon as his temple headquarters, was officially living in the territory that was initially his fathers, but had been transferred to Enlil as lord of the Command, focusing his efforts in and around Ur, Sippar, and Nippur.

Marduk wanted control of the space port located at Sippar and ultimately went to war with the Enlilites fighting over the tactically significant terrain. Eventually, Ninurta obtained a forbidden nuclear weapon hidden away in a cave and used it to destroy the space port when it became evident it could no longer be defended from the onslaught of the Marduk's attacks.

Interestingly, unbeknown to most, Abraham was an astute military general, working for Enlil. He was dispatched to Egypt to most likely spy on Enki's forces which landed in the Egyptian Nile Delta where he and his offspring were responsible for building the great pyramids which were used as navigational aids and energy generation and communication facilities. Abraham also came face to face with Marduk's forces in the vicinity of Haran, a city named after Abram's brother, also hailing from the Sumerian city of Ur.

In the final chapter, Zeus and Apollo assert themselves as the Father Son duo, the Great Destroyers. Who will they use as human fodder this time? With Zodiac houses changing to Aquarius, the Water Bearer's sign. Recall Enki/Poseidon was assigned control over the water. Lord of the Waters was his title given by Anu. The rising tides that suddenly buried Atlantis during the last earth changes, may be receding soon. According to top researchers, the New Atlantis is the planned headquarters for the New World Oder (NWO) [113].

12 ZEUS, APOLLO, AND THE NEW ATLANTIS

Prior to establishing the city of Atlantis, Enki and his Anunnaki gods on the council that declared mankind's fate, utilized the city of Baalbek, Lebanon as a space facility. It is here that the famed king Gilgamesh seeks an encounter with the gods in his initial quest for immortality, encountering the bull of heaven, which he and Enkidu, the genetic chimera, slew. Symbolically this is where the Anunnaki Council of 12 became the Greek Pantheon.

The Anunnaki, as a result of an all out nuclear onslaught on the Sinai peninsula circa 1600 BCE, left the region of Sumer, avoiding the "evil wind", or radioactive fallout as reported in the records. The Anunnaki Council of Twelve, effectively became the Greek Pantheon at Baalbek, moving Eastward towards the Greek peninsula to avoid the fallout of Ninurta's aerial destruction wrought on the Sinai space port [18].

Poseidon, as noted in the previous chapters, established the island nation of Atlantis, siring offspring that eventually landed in Greece. Poseidon and Zeus both had temples in Athens, Greece. It is well known that the Greek Pantheon was accepted as the state religion in Rome until Constantine opted to subsume the growing followers of Christ into a pagan aggregate, combining the birth of Jesus with the holiday of Saturnia on

December 23rd, currently recognized as December 25th, Christmas.

According to Wikipedia, Saturnalia was an ancient Roman festival in honor of the deity Saturn, the Greek equivalent of Cronus, held on December 17 of the Julian calendar and later expanded with festivities through December 23. The holiday was celebrated with a sacrifice at the Temple of Saturn in the Roman Forum and a public banquet, followed by private gift-giving, continual partying, and a carnival atmosphere that overturned Roman social norms: gambling was permitted, and masters provided table service for their slaves. Aliens would love Vegas!

Operating under the assumption that the deities of Sumeria were the same as those that occupied the mythological Greek Pantheon, we can create Table 9 that depicts the God's namesakes which spanned multiple cultures, maintaining their symbols and attributes in spite of the intentional changes to their hidden namesakes. Rob Solarian [38] provides several god tables that span other cultures as well. Note that it is sometimes very difficult to get the names exactly right given the hiding namesake practice.

Rank	Nibiru	Sumer	Egypt	Greece	Rome
60	Anu	Anshar	Geb/Seb	Cronus	Saturn
55	Antu	Nintu	Nut/Neith	Rhea	Ops
50	Enlil	Ashur		Zeus	Jupiter
45	Ninlil	Nammu	Ma'at	Maia	Majesta
40	Enki	Ea/Samael	Ptah	Poseidon	Neptune
??	??	Ningishzida	Thoth	Hermes	Mercury
15	Inanna	Ishtar	Hathor	Aphrodite	Venus
05	Ninharsag	Ninmah	Isis	Hera	Juno

Table 9: The God Table

Table 9 above, although in progress, should help the reader associate some of the names used for the gods of Sumeria with the names used in

Egypt, Rome and Greek mythology, the origins of Western civilization, as taught in American schools. This cross cultural link establishes the Anunnaki as the true power brokers behind the rise of the world's great civilizations, Mesopotamia, Egypt, and Greece to name just a few. They were also the authority vested in the rulers that wielded that power on behalf of the empire or kingdom.

According to the gospel author Paul, in his letter to the Greek church at Pergamum, it was the location of the seat of Satan in the Bible:

Revelation 2:12 (NIV)
"To the angel of the church in Pergamum write:
These are the words of him who has the sharp, double-edged sword. [13] I know where you live— where Satan has his throne. Yet you remain true to my name. You did not renounce your faith in me, not even in the days of Antipas, my faithful witness, who was put to death in your city—where Satan lives.

Thus, it seems we have tracked Angra Maiyu from his antagonistic role to Ahura Mazda from Persia to Greece, where the Biblical writers have established in writing that Satan has his throne in Pergamum. The Pergamum Altar is a massive structure originally built in the 2nd century BC in the Ancient Greek city of Pergamum. The temple was dedicated to the Greek god Zeus.

The Pergamum Altar was shipped out of the Ottoman Empire from the original excavation site by a German archeological team led by Carl

Humann, and reconstructed in the Pergamum Museum in Berlin in the 19th century. Zeus's Altar can be seen in the museum alongside other monumental structures such as the Ishtar Gate from Babylon.

Figure 19: Throne of Satan, Altar of Zeus

A mock up of the altar was designed for Obama's stage at the Democratic Nominating convention held at the mile high stadium in Denver, Colorado, 2008. Was Obama indicating through his choice of location and affiliation with Zeus, that he had been put in a role as United States President, which exposed him to the most highly classified information: namely confronting the reality of the Anunnaki presence on Earth, and the political ramifications thereof. Obama, as President would be serving Enlil as a puppet leader of the most powerful nation on the planet?

Revelations 9:11 (NIV)

They had as king over them the angel of the Abyss, whose name in Hebrew is Abaddon and in Greek is **Apollyon** (that is, Destroyer).

According to Tom Horn, author of "*Apollyon Rising 2012*" [113], Zeus and his Son Apollo would assert themselves as leaders of the New World

Order using the Catholic Church and the United States Presidency as the intended seats to be occupied by the father-son duo. Also, according to the Bible in Revelations 9:11, Apollo may have shared in the judgment to come, spoken of in the Lost Book of Enoch, as leader of the Igigi to be cast into the Abyss.

This Revelation prophecy formed the basis for the assertion that Apollo would be on the rise during the time that the New World Order was being established, as Tom Horn described, wreaking havoc and destruction with a spirit antithetical to that of Christ, along with his father, Zeus (Satan) who would perpetuate himself in the Christian Apocalyptic role as the False Prophet. According to Tom, Zeus would be promoted through the Catholic Church as the Pope, and Apollo would maneuver his way into controlling the reigns of the most powerful military on the planet, the United States of America. It remains to be seen whether Tom Horn was correct in his identification of the Anunnaki elites poised to bring about a New World Order. Given the symbology affiliated with the hidden power brokers of the world, coupled with the almost scripted fulfillment of Bible prophecy associated with Israel, it seems that the Anunnaki are returning as promised, with unknown consequences for mankind. If Zeus has his way expect a massive reduction in the human population. Consider the forces of creation and destruction represented by Enki and Enlil. From Anu's perspective, both are needed. This is hard to grasp, but creation and destruction have to be in balance to maintain homeostasis. Thu, seeing the fact that the half-brothers cooperate is analogous to God and the Devil playing a board game for the conquest of mankind's soul. The epic battle between dark and light, good and evil.

Could Apollo be the "Angel in the Whirlwind" referred to by former president George W. Bush, in a speech he gave as a prelude to the unleashing of destructive forces in the Iraq Gulf war and subsequent middle east turmoil, riots, and upheavals as seen in the "*Arab Spring*".

In the interim period, between governmental disclosure of the Anunnaki alien presence on earth, and the build up to World War III, mankind is trapped between the fates declared by their Niburian gods and the perceived freedom to pursue life, liberty, and happiness as the New Atlantis arises before our very eyes.

Canada's former Defense minister, Paul Hellyer, is going viral on YouTube, testifying to the United States Congress about alien astronauts which he had direct knowledge of in his official capacity.

In his YouTube video released on July 24th, 2013 [https://www.youtube.com/watch?v=Lu5V8gqFQ1c], Paul mentions up to 20 alien species that have been here, some for thousands of years, hailing from Zeta Reticuli, Pleiades, Orion, Andromeda Galaxy and the Altair Star Systems, while reading from his book "Light at the End of the Tunnel: A Survival Plan for the Human Species". Although, Paul does not mention Nibiru or the Anunnaki, to my knowledge.

Paul makes particular mention about aliens occupying a base near Indian Springs, Nevada, guarded by United States Air Force personnel where he discusses two alien "Tall Whites" working with the United States Government. These entities are most likely Zeus and Apollo, as predicted by Tom Horn and the Biblical Revelations reference to Apollyon being the demon leader.   Paul Hellyer spent 23 years in the Canadian government finalizing his career as the minister of defense.   His assertion is that the universe is teeming with a variety of intelligent life forms, some far more advanced than we are, and they are interacting with us shaping world events as claimed in this book, from the beginning of recorded time.

In the Christian tradition, the faithful hold out the hope for the return of the messiah Jesus, to bring the heavenly (Niburian) kingdom to Earth (like Eridu?)   When the three wise men of the East, namely dispatched astrologers from Ahura Mazda's Persia, were sent with kingly gifts for Jesus-Ningishzida at birth, it should force one to ask the question why Magi from Iran, Enki's domain, were traveling to an area controlled by Enlil's Roman governors and Jewish priests loyal to the god of wrath and vengeance, Jehovah himself?   *It should be obvious to the reader that is was Enki interceding on behalf of mankind, just as he did earlier in the Atrahasis account in Mesopotamia and Africa, countering the oppressive beat-down his brother had planned for the noisy humans.*

Suppression of Human Consciousness, a tenet that Enlil strongly supported relative to the primitive workers fashioned by Enki and his half-sister Ninharsag in Africa, was a concept closely tied to slavery, purportedly outlawed on Nibiru.   Recall that consciousness had the stinging side effect of empowering the enslaved to rise up casting off their oppressors, not an acceptable slave behavior under Enlil's command.   Enki was far more sympathetic to the human cause, rightly so as their genetic creator.   Thus, it should not surprise the reader to find that Jesus' bloodline was connected to Enki, not Enlil.   There are many instances in the Sumerian record in which Enki subverts the authority and command of Enlil, much to his angry chagrin. This is why the Jews reject Jesus as the messiah: their god Enlil could never accept a genetic representative of Enki as mankind's vehicle out of a terminally suppressed consciousness. Jesus threw mankind a rope on behalf of the Enkiites, providing a means to continue their spiritual evolution as Enki believe the Creator of All intended.

Consider the dying and rising god rituals that were frequently conducted in Egypt, Enki's domain. A significant country and god list showing that the ritual was conducted across a broad region was noted. The point of the ritual, according to Wikipedia, was to dispense a frequency from the departing god which was used to elevate human consciousness to that of the departing/dying god. Compare the language used in the Bible with the concept just described.

John 1:12 (NIV)

Yet to all who did receive him, to those who believed in his name, he gave the right to become children of God.

Note the general idea of receiving a "frequency" or "power" that is latent, imposing the responsibility of "becoming" or transforming into Enki's genetic archetype. This subtle reference holds the key to the internal kingdom of Nibiru/Heaven. It is the author's direct experience that the latent energy referenced by Jesus-Thoth is fully described in detail in the Emerald Tablets. Additionally, the concept of transformation or becoming implies action that must be taken by the frequency recipient. It is the author's personal contention, that becoming involves releasing the latent Kundalini energy allocated by the dying god frequency stored in the Ganglion of Impar (in the Sacrum) and aligning the human body with the gravity field so that equation [EQ5A] is realized. At this point, the Caduceus of Thoth-Jesus will make more empirical sense to the reader.

Thus, Jesus-Thoth taught that if one were to receive the "frequency" being dispensed by his death, that it had the power to transform the primitive workers, whose consciousness had been repeatedly repressed by the Enlilites, occupying the Levantine with Pontius Pilate as the acting Governor. He was the judge at Jesus' trial, and authorized his crucifixion. So what did it mean to become a child of God? Could it be related to an internal change in human energy and consciousness, achieving the knowledge of good and evil as Enlil sought to withhold from the first primitive workers that Enki had brought to the Eridu garden of ED.IN (the Biblical Eden), where they were being observed to ensure that the procreative genetic upgrade provided by Enki's son Ningishzida-Thoth, were effective? Did Jesus-Thoth allude to the seven chakras being blocked, when he spoke of casting out the seven demons from Mary Magdalene in Mark 16:1? It would make sense, if, where the finite meets the infinite, where energy meets matter, we find the kingdom of God within you as Jesus stated in the Gospels as measurable energy along the Chakras.

According to a website article sponsored by the United Church of God, "Is the Kingdom of God within you?", many people believe Jesus Christ taught that the Kingdom of God is something that exists only in the hearts and minds of believers. They base this on the Bible verse:

Luke 17:20-21: (NIV)

"Now when He was asked by the Pharisees when the kingdom of God would come, He answered them and said, 'The kingdom of God does *not come with observation; nor will they say, 'See here!' or 'See there!' For indeed, the kingdom of God is within you.'"*

The article takes issue with this statement, explaining that the assumption that the Kingdom only exists in the hearts of believers was incorrect, as the correct Greek translation for the word entos, within is better translated "in the midst of". This is a pivotal distinction, rather than Christianity being a concept in their hearts, Jesus was warning them that they were so spiritually blind that they could not recognize God in him, the future king of an Earthly rulership, according to the article [119].

The author emphatically disagrees with the United Church stance. Given our knowledge of the electromagnetic spectrum and the human body whose structure and function provide mechanisms for mankind's Anunnaki enslavement and ascension, Thoth-Jesus' frequency dispensation allow the chosen to pass through the narrow gates of the righteous rules of the rocket ship from Nibiru, bypassing Enlil's glass ceiling. Thoth-Ningishzida's emblem was the famed healer's Caduceus. This symbol of the serpent and the Tree of Knowledge are represented in the insignia of the American and British medical associations. The brain's pineal gland was directly associated with the Tree of Life by the ancient Greeks. Two coiled serpents (DNA double helix) wrapped around a central winged pole, with a knob on top (pineal gland) had significant meaning relative to energy and matter, associated with the messenger-god, Mercury-Hermes-Ningishzida, thrice born. The central staff represents the spinal cord and the nerve ganglia distributed at the seven discrete Chakras. The wings represent the brain's lateral ventricles, with the pineal represented as a unary ball on top of the central pole. The combination of the central pineal gland, coupled with the lateral wings, is sometimes referred to in the Yoga tradition as the Swan of full enlightenment.

Mystery schools located along the Nile River were administered by Thoth-Hermes, whose primary goal was teaching students the process for achieving enlightened consciousness. The process of activating the potential Kundalini energy in the sacrum, and its wiggling snake-like movement from the bottom of the central pole at the end of the coccyx bone (defined as the Ganglion of Impar, which is purported to be the negative pole of the energy body) upwards to the crown Chakra collocated with the pineal gland, triggering a DMT release and an elevated consciousness as indicated by wings of flight.

Jesus spoke of casting out seven demons and called people stiff-necked in the New Testament. Given our discussion of the fallen state of mankind, specifically referring to Structural Integration and the extent to which human fascia naturally stiffens as we age, could the term mean a physical problem, or stubbornness, or are the two related? Is this derogatory label used for the primitive workers, calling them "stiff-necked", used by the Anunnaki elite, namely Enlil, given his influence in rewriting the Sumerian tales by captive Hebrew Priests dedicated to appeasing his wrath in the Torah. The God of the Old Testament Bible uses the term 10 times as documented here.

Exodus 32:9, 33:3, 33:5, 34:9

Deuteronomy 9:6, 9:13, 10:16 and Deuteronomy 31:27

GERALD R. CLARK

2 Kings 17:14 and 2 Chronicles 30:8

Note that human fascia loses moisture, or ground substance as it is termed in the Structural Integration, with age, the collagen hardening like bone in some folks. This is a keen observation Enlil makes, noting a potential defect in his arch rival Enki's primitive worker physical design. Apparently, as witnessed in the global population of humans and their relationship to gravity, we see that the connective tissue hardens over time without intervention, leading to various medical labels to include Fibromyalgia. Western Medicine, along with academia, the government and the military have been infiltrated and taken over by NWO forces. Thus, don't expect to get well in the current health care system, and those services that will truly get you healthy are not covered by insurance. Previous Fibromyalgia SI clients were counseled to avoid the work by their Western medicine primary care providers, opting instead to play the role of pharmacologist versus actual healer. True healers like Dr. Robert Fulford, D.O. are few and far between. His 60-year practice as an old time osteopathic doctor is evolved and inspiring. See his book "Robert Fulford, D.O. And the Philosopher Physician", Eastland Press, 2002.

To finalize the discussion on whether the Kingdom of Nibiru, I mean Heaven, is within the energy body of human, a further look at the Chakra system and the antagonistic position many Christian organizations have taken relative to the organized stretching system is now discussed, again, for the last time I hope.

Suppose for a moment that the blockages in the human body that impede the Chakras from working have to do with an unstructured body (subluxation is a term often used by Chiropractors) in the gravity field, as Ida Rolf indicated in her seminal book [6]. Given the fact that Jesus spent

30 or so years unaccounted for studying in Egypt, likely as a student at the Thoth's mystery school according to historical records, Enki's domain, where the scientists were esteemed. Let's call the blockages demons and then follow along.

Mary Magdalene was Thoth-Jesus' best student and most highly esteemed disciple. If Jesus had cleared her seven Chakras, or seven demons as Mark and Luke record in the New Testament accounts, then it is possible that she had already been transformed into a higher level Anunnaki consciousness, more on par with Jesus-Ningizhzida. It is no wonder he preferred her company over that of the other disciples whose consciousness was still most likely at Root Chakra level. Some pretty radical thinking about Chakras and the casting out of demons is evidence of this un-evolved belief by some Christians.

Figure 20: Hindu Chakras, Colors, Gods

According to some sources, the "demons" that are blocking the

Chakras are affiliated with the Hindu religion. Based on the response of the Demoniac in the tomb setting that Jesus encounters in the Gospels, he says that the name of the demon is Legion, and we are many. Could these "demons" be the Igigi that were given a judgment of destruction at the end times, according the Book of Enoch. The demon asks if Jesus has come to judge him before the appointed time, which is when exactly? Interesting coincidence here. There is a distinct battle ground that has formed between some religions and the human nerve ganglia, the Chakras as shown. For clarification, listed below are the Chakras, their colors, and the Hindu affiliated Gods that have a cork stopper stuck in your ganglia from birth, according to some... What follows is a link to the source material. http://www.lotussculpture.com/blog/chakras-colors-hindu-gods/ by Kyle Tortora, Nov 2, 2012.

Chakras , Colors, Biology, and Hindu Deity:

1. **Muladhara**: The Root Chakra – located at base of the spine. Associated with the color red. It affects confidence, trust in life and self-esteem. It is from here that our base instincts arise; the need to survive or the fight or flight reflex. Chakra is controlled by Hindu God –Lord Ganesh and Brahman.

2. Swadhisthana: The Sacral Chakra – located below the navel. Associated with the color orange. It affects sexual desires, attractions and the need to procreate. Other emotions such as, anger, fear and hatred stem from this chakra. Chakra is controlled by Hindu God –Lord Vishnu

3. **Manipura**: The Solar Plexus Chakra – located at the bottom of the breast bone. Associated with bright yellow. It affects the lower back, digestive system, liver and gall bladder. Feelings that are associated with this chakra, include, determination, self-acceptance and will power. It is here that instinctual emotion translates to more complex emotions. Chakra is controlled by Hindu God –Maharudra Shiva

4. **Anahata**: The Heart Chakra – located at the center of the chest. Associated with green. Feelings associated with this location are love, compassion, emotional security, forgiveness and loving kindness. Chakra is controlled by Hindu God –Ishvara

5. **Vishuddha**: The Throat Chakra – located at the throat, over the larynx. Associated with the color blue. It is the source of our ability to communicate, and express creativity and individuality. Controlled by the Hindu God – Sadashiva

6. **Ajna**: The Third Eye Chakra – located at front of the head in between eye brows. Associated with color indigo. The mind, as the sense organ and action organ are associated with this chakra. Feelings associated with this chakra are spirituality, awareness, and sense of time. Hindu God - Ardhanarishvara –an androgynous form of Hindu god Lord Shiva and Parvati, also known as Devi and Shakti

7. **Sahasrara**: The Crown Chakra – located at the top of the head, the pineal gland. Associated with purple, or gold. It is from this Chakra that all others emanate. It relates to pure consciousness. In Hindu literature, it is known as "the supreme center of contact with God." Here liberated ones

abide in communion with the Self. Chakra is controlled by Hindu God –
Lord Shiva

It is the author's personal experience that ethical-righteous behavior is
a fruit of the spirit achieved by those brave enough and disciplined enough
to relate their bodies to the gravity field. The mystical "Rolf Line",
representing a human aligned to the gravity field fulfilling equation
[EQ5/EQ5A] shown in Chapter 6, represents the maximal human energy.
This energy or spirit as it is called in religious organizations, coincides with
the highest intelligence imparted by the creators: both the Creator of All as
termed by the Anunnaki, and the premier genetic scientist, the far-sighted
Enki, putting his personal *stamp* on the primitive worker Adapa, the first
modern man. A very unique stamp was placed on the primitive workers:
seven nerve ganglia aligned in ascending order, partitioning of the visible
spectrum into seven discretely quantized wavelength specific (rainbow-
colored) Chakras imparted to his unique creation: the primitive workers of
the seventh planet, now called Earth. Seven was a lucky number for good
reason, as promoted by the Anunnaki. Seven times Seven has even more
significance it seems, at least for me. That is the biological age at which I
finally got this book to print, nine years in the making.

Thoth states in the Emerald Tablets that he lived three incarnations.
Could one of the incarnations have been played out as the bringer of
salvation to the primitive workers, living as Enlil's pawns protecting a
transportation portal which they know nothing about, in the land promised
to Abraham. Subversive tactical births seeding a genetic war against his half
brother Enlil were being played out in Jerusalem, right beneath his nose.
What better way for Enki to make up for a genetic enslavement decision
imposed on mankind, approved by the Anunnaki Council in Africa, than to

freely make an energetic frequency-based mechanism available to his creation, that by simply believing in a name, had the power to transform the intentionally dumbed-down genetic underlings designed to mine gold, into the "Sons of God", allowing the evolution of consciousness to proceed unabated according the genetic seed in mankind, designed by the Creator of All.

Given that Enki's genetic material was used to create the first Adapa, the transformation promised by Jesus-Thoth-Ningishzida, to become a son or daughter of "God" may be one originally ingeniously contrived by his father Enki, to allow mankind to continue on its course to becoming a full-blown, genetically freed Niburian archetypal citizen, a son of Enki or a daughter of Isis, for the lucky ones destined to partake of the bread and waters of eternal life, whose access is closely guarded by those who from Nibiru to Earth came..

BIBLIOGRAPHY

1. Strassman, Dr. Rick, "DMT The Spirit Molecule"

2. Stephen W. Hawking, "The Future of Spacetime"

3. Jared Diamond , "Guns, Germs and Steel: The Fates of Human Societies"

4. Food of the Gods, Terence McKenna

5. Transformation, Robert A. Johnson

6. Rolfing: Reestablishing the Natural Alignment and Structural Integration of the Human Body for Vitality and Well-Being, Ida P. Rolf, Ph.D.

7. Structure is Function and Energy, Gerald Clark

8. The Sivananda Companion to Yoga, Swami Vishnu Devananda

9. The Templar Revelation: Secret Guardians of the True Identity of Christ, Clive Prince and Lynn Picknett

10. Dan Brown, "The DaVinci Code"

11. Wolf, "Physics, Extended with Modern Physics"

12. Serway, Moses, and Moyer, "Modern Physics"

13. Sitchin, Zecharia, "Genesis Revisited"

14. Sitchin, Zecharia, The Lost Book of Enki

15. Sitchin, Zecharia, Divine Encounters, A guide to Visions, Angels, and Other Emissaries,

16. Sitchin, Zecharia, The Earth Chronicles Book 1: The 12th Planet,

17. Sitchin, Zecharia, The Earth Chronicles Book 2: The Stairway to Heaven,

18. Sitchin, Zecharia, The Earth Chronicles Book 3: The Wars of Gods and Men,

19. Sitchin, Zecharia, The Earth Chronicles Book 4: The Lost Realms

20. Sitchin, Zecharia, The Earth Chronicles Book 5: When Time Began

21. Sitchin, Zecharia, "The Earth Chronicles Book 6: The Cosmic Code"

22. Sitchin, Zecharia, "The Earth Chronicles Expeditions: Journeys to the Mythical Past"

23. Tolle, Eckhard, "The Power of Now"

24. LaViolette, "Genesis of the Cosmos"

25. Young, Arthur, "Geometry of Meaning"

26. Young, Arthur "Reflexive Universe",

27. Holographic Universe, Michael Talbot

28. McCutcheon, Mark , "The Final Theory"

29. Drosnin, Michael, "Bible Code I"

30. Drosnin Michael, "Bible Code II, The Countdown"

31. And the truth shall set you free, David Icke

32. Ancient Secrets of the Flower of Life Vols 1, Drumvalo Melchizedek

33. Ancient Secrets of the Flower of Life Vol 2, Drumvalo Melchizedek

34. The Hidden Messages in Water, Dr. Masasru Emoto

35. Living in the Heart, Drumvalo Melchizedek

36. The Lost Book of Enoch, Joseph Lumpkin, 2004.

37. Dalley, Stephanie, "Myths From Mesopotamia Creation, The Flood, Gilgamesh, and Others", 2000, Oxford University Press

38. Osiris, Isis, & Planet X Chasing the Centuries, Rob Solarion, 2006, Authorhouse

39. Edgar Cayce Modern Prophet, Random House Publishing, 1990

40. Abraham The First Historical Biography, David Rosenberg, Basic Books, 2006

41. Gods, Demons, and Symbols of Ancient Mesopotamia, Jeremy Black and Anthony Green, University of Texas, 2003

42. 2012 The Return of Quetzalcoatl, Daniel Pinchbeck, The Penguin Group, 2006

43. Kramer, Samuel Noah, "History Begins at Sumer: Thirty-Nine First in Recorded History", University of Pennsylvania Press, 1981

44. The Nephilim And the Pyramid of the Apocalypse, Patrick Heron, Xulon Press, 2005

45. Astrology: Understanding the Birth Chart, Kevin Burk, Llewellyn Publishing, 2003

46. Teresi, Dick, "Lost Discoveries", , Simon & Schuster, 2002

47. Woods, Michael and Mary, "Ancient Transportation, from Camels to Canals", Runestone Press, 2000

48. Gardner, Laurence, "Genesis of the Grail Kings", Barnes and Noble, 2004

49. Zeinert, Karen, "The Persian Empire, Cultures of the Past", Benchmark Books, New York, 1997.

50. Pamela F. Service, "Mesopotamia: Cultures of the Past", Benchmark Books, New York, 1999.

51. Don Nardo, Empires of Mesopotamia: Lost Civilizations, Lucent Books, San Diego, 2001.

52. Marsh, Ross, ID'sI: Salah of Genisis is Belk-Marduk, www.domainofman.com, May 2001

53. Henry, William, "The Blue Stones of Atlantis Ireland and the Lost Tribe of E.A."
http://williamhenry.net/documents/blue_stones_of_alantis.pdf

54. Schoville, Keith N., "Top Ten Archaeological Discoveries of the Twentieth Century Relating to the Biblical World", http://biblicvalstudies.infor/top10/schoville.htm

55. "A Mesopotamian Pantheon", http://web.raex.com/~obsidian/MesoPan.html

56. D.M, "Nibiru and the Anunnaki", 2002, http://www.cyberspaceorbit.com/dm_report.html

57. Reconstructing the Pantheon, http://home.nycap.rr.comn/foxmob/sumer_pantheon03.htm

58. Survey and Excavation Projects in Egypt (SEPE), South Sinai, El-Markha 1, Mumford, Dr. Gregory, University of Toronto, Http://www.deltasinai.com/sinai-01.htm

59. Jaeger, John, "Anunnaki and Nibiru the Return", http://www.pufoin.com/pufoin_perspective/nibiru.php

60. "Gods Explore", http://www.mesopotamia.co.uk/gods/explore

61. "Thule Society-Crystalinks", http://www.crystalinkks.com/thule.html

62. Sitchin, Zecharia, "Dialogue in Bellaria", http://www.sitchin.com/vatical.htm

63. Roug, Louise, "Digitizing Cuneiform", LA Times, http:///www.ancientsites.com/aw/Post/148092

64. "Curious About Astronomy", http://curious.astro.cornell.edu/

65. Meij, Harold, "Trestleboards", 1998, http://www3tky.3web.ne.jp/

66. Calleman, Carl Johan, "The Mayan Calendar and the Transformantion of Consciousness", Bear & Co., 2004.

67. "Mayan Calendar II", http://www.exeriencefestival.com/a/Mayan_Clanedar/id/1724

68. Rewcknagel, Charles, "Iraq: Archaeological Expedition Mapping Ancient City of Uruk",
http://www.rferl.org/features/2002/05/03052002101632.asp

69. The Threat to World heritage in Iraq,
http://users.ox.ac.uk/~wolf0126/

70. Baalbek-Lebanon's Sacred Fortress, Andrew Collins,
http://www.andrewcollins.com/pages/articles/baalbek.htm

71. Twelve Olympians,
http://en.wikipedia.org/wiki/Twelve_Olympians

72. Ancient Astronauts Reading List, Alan F. Alford,
http://www.eridu.co.uk/Author/human_origins/AAS_Intro2/Reading/reading.html

73. Edgar Cayce, The body-Temple of God,
http://www.edgarcayce.org/s2/body_temple_of_god_J_Van_Auken.html

74. Gilgamesh Tomb Believed Found,
http://newsvote.bbc.co.uk/mpapps/pagetools/print/news.bbc.co.uk/2/hi/science/nature/2982891.stm, 04.29.03 BBC News.

75. Dr. Michael E. Salla, Feb. 2003, "Stargate War: An Exopolitical Perspective On The Preemptive War Against Iraq",
www.exopolitics.org

76. White, Paul, "The Secrets of Thoth and the Keys of Enoch",
http://www.lightparty.com/Spirituality/ThothEnoch.html

77. "In the Beginning", 2005,
http://members.aol.com/jimb3d/myth/genesis2.html

78. ISIS Regina Caeli, http://www.maat.it/livello2-i/iside-01-i.htm

79. Pagan Goddess of the Sibyl and Cybele Oracle,
    http:///www.goddess.org/vortices/notes/cybele.html

80. Pagan Goddess Mytstical Rites- An Introduction, by MaatRaAh,
    http://www.goddess.org/vortices/index.html

81. A Brief History of the Planet Nibiru, Robert Solarion, 1996,
    http://www.god-forum.co.za/English/articles/nibiru.htm

82. Freer, Neil "The Annunaki and the Myth of a 12th Planet", 2006, ,
    http://www.red-ice.net/specialreports/2006/01jan/annunaki.html

83. The Annunaki, Estelle Nora Harwit Amrani, August 3, 2000
    http://www.vibranni.com/Annunaki.htm

84. http://www.haarp.alaska.edu/haarp/tech.html

85. Smith, Jerry E., "HAARP: The ultimate Weapon of the
    Conspiracy", 2003, Adventures Unlimied Press, pages 10-20.

86. Powledge, Tabitha, "The Great DNA Hunt", Archeology Volume
    49 Number 5, Sept/Oct 1996.
    http://www.archaeology.org/9609/abstracts/dna.html

87. http://en.wikipedia.org/wiki/Out_of_Africa_theory

88. Chew, Freeland, "Zecharia Sitchin and a New Synthesis",
    http://www.banned-
    books.com/1997archive/124_1/36_zecharia.html

89. Enuma Elish, http://www.sacred-texts.com/ane/enuma.htm

90. MacLean, Paul. *The Triune Brain in Evolution: Role in Paleocerebral
    Functions* (Plenum, 1990, ISBN 0306431688).

91. A.k.a. basal ganglia or extrapyramidal motor system. Panksepp,
    Jaak. *Affective Neuroscience: The Foundations of Human and Animal
    Emotions* (Oxford, 1998, ISBN 0-19-509673-8), p. 42.

92. Lewis, T., Amini, F., Lannon, R. *A General Theory of Love* (Random House, 2000, ISBN 0375503897), 25-26.

93. Callaway, Jace, "A proposed mechanism of rhte visions of dream sleep, "Medical Hypotheses 26, 1988: 119-24.

94. Machiavelli, Nicolo, "The Prince", c 1505.

95. Abrams, D.B., & Wilson, G.T. (1979). Effects of alcohol on social anxiety in women: Cognitive versus physiological processes. *Journal of Abnormal Psychology*, 88, 161-173.

96. Banaji, M.R., & Steele, C.M. (1989). The social cognition of alcohol use. *Social Cognition*, 7, 137-151.

97. Josephs, R.A., & Steele, C.M. (1990). The two faces of alcohol myopia: Attentional mediation of psychological stress. *Journal of Abnormal Psychology*, 99, 115-126.

98. Keane, T.M., & Lisman, S.A. (1980). Alcohol and social anxiety in males: Behavioral, cognitive, and physiological effects. *Journal of Abnormal Psychology*, 89, 213-223.

99. Levenson, R.W., Sher, K.J., Grossman, L.M., Newman, J., & Newlin, D.B. (1980). Alcohol and stress response dampening: Pharmacological effects, expectancy, and tension reduction. *Journal of Abnormal Psychology*, 89, 528-538.

100. MacDonald, T.K., Zanna, M.P., & Fong, G.T. (1996). Why common sense goes out the window: Effects of alcohol on intentions to use condoms. *Personality and Social Psychology Bulletin*, 22, 763-775.

101. Murphy, S.T., Monahan, J.L., & Miller, L.C. (1998). Inference under the influence: The impact of alcohol and inhibition conflict on women's sexual decision making. *Personality and Social Psychology Bulletin*, 24, 517-528.

102. Polivy, J., Schueneman, A.L., & Carlson, K. (1976). Alcohol and tension reduction: Cognitive and physiological effects. *Journal of Abnormal Psychology,* 85, 595-600.

103. Steele, C.M., Critchlow, B., & Liu, T.J. (1985). Alcohol and social behavior: 2. The helpful drunkard. *Journal of Personality and Social Psychology,* 48, 35-46.

104. Steele, C.M., & Josephs, R.A. (1988). Drinking your troubles away: 2. An attention-allocation model of alcohol's effect on psychological stress. *Journal of Abnormal Psychology,* 97, 196-205.

105. Steele, C.M., & Josephs, R.A. (1990). Alcohol myopia: It's prized and dangerous effects. *American Psychologist,* 363-375.

106. Zeichner, A., & Phil, R.O. (1979). Effects of alcohol and behavior contingencies on human aggression. *Journal of Abnormal Psychology,* 88, 153- 160.

107. Zeichner, A., & Phil, R.O. (1980). Effects of alcohol and instigator intent on human aggression. *Journal of Studies on Alcohol,* 41, 265-276.

108. Hapgood, Charles H. (1958). Earth's Shifting Crust: A Key to Some Basic Problems of Earth Science. New York: Pantheon Books.

109. Balick, B., Brown, R.L., 1974, *Intense Sub-arcsecond Structure in the Galactic Center,* Astrophysical Journal 194, p 265.

110. GMO Pig Study
http://www.pri.org/stories/science/environment/study-finds-health-issues-with-pigs-consuming-genetically-modified-foods-14195.html

111. Heine, Johan & Tellinger, Michael, "Adam's Calendar:

Discovering the Oldest man-made Structure on Earth-75,0000 years ago." , 2008.

112. United Church of God, "Is the Kingdom of God *within you*"?, http://www.ucg.org/bible-faq/kingdom-god-within-you

113. Horn, Tom, "Apollyon Rising 2012: The Lost Symbol Found and the Final Mystery of the Great Seal Revealed", Defender, 2009, signed copy by Tom!!! Future congress, Branson MO.

114. Hansen, L. Tayler, "The Ancient Atlantic", Library of Congress, and Amherst Press, 1969.

115. Isaac, encyclopedia of Islam, Vol. 4: Qur'an , XXXVII 100-107

116. Hilprecht, H.V. "The Babylonian Expedition of the University of Pennsylvania: Series A: Cuneiform Texts", Vol VI, Part 1. Dept of Archeology, University of Pennsylvania, 1906.

117. Guild for Structural Integration www.rolfguild.org

118. Kunkle, Parke, "Ophiuchus, new Zodiac Sign Dates and Your Real Astrological Sign", 2011, http://blog.zap2it.com/pop2it/2011/01/ophiuchus-new-zodiac-sign-dates-and-your-real-astrological-sign.html

119. Tellinger, Michael, "Slave Species of God", Bear and Co., 2005.

INDEX

APPENDIX A: GENEALOGY TABLES

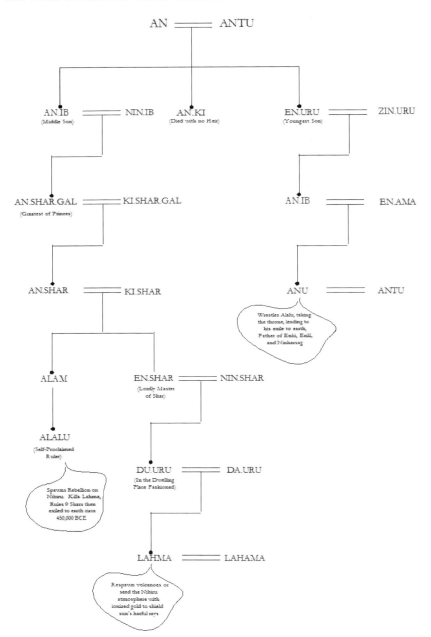

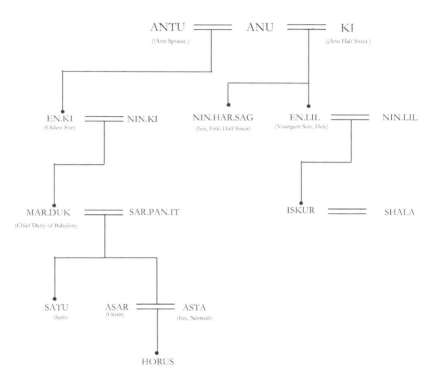

A complete Genealogy table beginning with a pre-history on Nibiru, down through the Babylonian Epic of Creation, including the Sumerian King's List, integrated with the very excellent table authored by Laurence Gardner, page 316 of "Genesis of the Grail Kings" depicting the Grand Assembly of the Anunnaki, is available by serious inquiry only. Email me.

ABOUT THE AUTHOR

Gerald Clark is a 1994 graduate of the University of California at San Diego holding an MSEE in Electronic Circuits and Systems and a BS in Computer Engineering. Gerald is the author of several papers in the communications and electronics field and is well known for his work in the San Diego high technology industry, awarded several patents in the Free Space Optical Laser Communications Field while serving as Vice President of Engineering, LightPointe Communications, Inc. Gerald's career involved companies like Loral Telemetry and Instrumentation where he lead the final design phase of the Globalstar Telemetry and Command Modem designed for Qualcomm- designed to command, monitor, and control 54 LEO Satellites.

While serving as VP Engineering at Tiernan Communications, Gerald and his small team of hardware and software engineers were credited with "Digitizing American Television", having demonstrated the first live HDTV Monday night football game on-air transmission from New York to the world using Tiernan Communications, Inc. HDTV 720p MPEG-2 Encoders.

During the years 1996-2002, working as a telecommunications executive, Gerald's business travels took him to various parts of the world exposing him to a plethora of cultures which acted as a catalyst for his research in the earliest technologies and accomplishments including the cultures of Mesopotamia and the surrounding areas of Turkey, Egypt, Persia, and Iraq, eventually leading to the cuneiform inscribed tablets left by the Sumerians.

As a Chief Warrant Officer (CWO2) and helicopter pilot in the United States Army, 1982-1989, Gerald's duties included night vision goggle and instrument trainer as well as acting as the unit's master fitness trainer. Gerald obtained his commercial rotary wing instrument ticket and approximately 1500 flight hours in both AH-1S Cobra and OH-58 Kiowa helicopters and served overseas in South Korea and Germany.

Knowledge of the Anunnaki here on Earth, both in the ancient past their presence here and now, is being fully-disclosed around the world. My hope is that this book will help the billions of primitive workers, left to fend for themselves on a hostile planet, to find hope that following the great destruction underway, wrought by the warring gods of Light and Dark, a promised peace in the new age of Aquarius is dawning, actually already upon us.

I am excited about sharing this research with like-minded collaborators authors, film makers, and seekers of the truth. Contact me via email at:

clark.gerald7@gmail.com

Be ye kind and of good integrity, most of all animate the frequency of

Love, the one devised by the Creator of All for us to enjoy. Best wishes on your quests and I look forward to hearing from you.